The Honourable James Jacob Spigelman AC holds Arts and Law degrees from the University of Sydney. From 1972 he was Senior Advisor and Principal Private Secretary to Prime Minister Whitlam, before being appointed as Permanent Secretary of the Department of Media in 1975. He served as a member of the Law Reform Commission, then commenced practice at the NSW Bar in 1980. He was appointed as Queen's Counsel in 1986 and Acting Solicitor General of NSW in 1997. He was appointed as Chief Justice of NSW and Lieutenant Governor in 1998.

Prior to his appointment as Chief Justice, he was on the boards of a range of public institutions devoted to the arts and education. He is the author of *Secrecy* (1972), *Becket and Henry* (2004) and co-author of *The Nuclear Barons* (1981).

THE **MCPHERSON LECTURE** SERIES

Statutory Interpretation and Human Rights

James Spigelman

VOLUME THREE

UQP

First published 2008 by University of Queensland Press
PO Box 6042, St Lucia, Queensland 4067 Australia

www.uqp.com.au

Typeset in 12/16.5pt Bembo by Post Pre-press Group, Brisbane
Printed in Australia by McPherson's Printing Group

Produced with the assistance of the TC Beirne School of Law at the University of Queensland.

Cataloguing-in-Publication Data
National Library of Australia

Spigelman, James, 1946-

Statutory interpretation and human rights / The Hon. James Jacob Spigelman, AC.

McPherson lecture series: v v. 3.
Includes index.

9780702236877 (pbk.)

Human rights
Civil rights
Law – Interpretation and construction

340.1

CONTENTS

PREFACE

In 2005, the TC Beirne School of Law at the University of Queensland decided to establish a new annual lecture series. The series was to be named in honour of one of Queensland's, and Australia's, finest judges, the Hon. Mr Justice Bruce McPherson of the Queensland Court of Appeal. That decision was particularly fitting given the Judge's association with the School, as both a member of the teaching faculty early on in his career and as a PhD graduate of the School. The School was delighted when Lord Millett accepted its invitation to give the first series of lectures, and these were delivered in March 2006. Lord Millett's lectures were published by UQP under the title *On Villainy.* The second series of lectures was delivered by Professor Peter Cane of the Australian National

University in March 2007. These lectures, which further underlined Professor Cane's outstanding scholarship in this area, were published as the second volume in the present series under the title *The Political Economy of Personal Injury Law.*

The 2008 McPherson Lectures were delivered by the Hon. James Spigelman, Chief Justice of New South Wales. The lectures, now presented in this book, address the subject of the interrelationship of the common law principles of statutory interpretation and developing notions of human rights, particularly in the context of formal bills of rights. The lectures were once again held in the Banco Court at the Supreme Court of Queensland. The TC Beirne School of Law gratefully acknowledges once more the generous support of the Hon. Paul de Jersey, Chief Justice of Queensland. The School continues to be grateful to Madonna Duffy and her team at the University of Queensland Press for embracing the concept of publishing this annual series.

Ross Grantham
Professor of Commercial Law
Head and Dean, TC Beirne School of Law
University of Queensland

THE COMMON LAW BILL OF RIGHTS

CHAPTER ONE

THE COMMON LAW BILL OF RIGHTS

Introduction

I am honoured by your invitation to deliver the 2008 McPherson Lectures. Bruce McPherson is one of the outstanding Australian lawyers of my time in the law. I have long admired his legal scholarship and his judgments, particularly as a judge of an intermediate court of appeal. They are always learned, closely reasoned and definitive in their exposition of the area of the law with which his Honour was then concerned. As counsel I always felt that I was lucky to have anything Bruce McPherson said in my favour. As a judge I have invariably found his writing illuminating and instructive. His legal career fully deserved the rare honour of a Festschrift in which the length, depth and quality of his contribution to the law is set forth.[1]

The theme I have chosen for the 2008 McPherson Lectures is statutory interpretation and human rights.[2] The first lecture will concentrate on the group of principles of the law of statutory interpretation which constitute, in substance, a common law bill of rights.[3] The second lecture will be concerned with the application of quasi-constitutional laws such as a statutory bill of rights and the common law bill of rights. How are the principles of statutory interpretation applied to legislation of this character? The third lecture will consider the limits of interpretation, distinguishing genuine from spurious interpretation.

One of the ways that the multifaceted process referred to as 'globalisation' has been manifest in world legal systems

---

1 Aladin Rahemtula (ed), *Justice According to Law: A Festschrift for the Honourable Mr Justice B H McPherson CBE* (2006) Supreme Court of Queensland Library, Brisbane.

2 These lectures involve a re-presentation and development of ideas put forward in earlier addresses: see JJ Spigelman, 'Statutory Interpretation: Identifying the Linguistic Register' (1999) 4 *Newcastle Law Review* 1; JJ Spigelman, 'The Poet's Rich Resource: Issues in Statutory Interpretation' (2001) 21 *Australian Bar Review* 224; JJ Spigelman, 'Blackstone, Burke, Bentham and the *Human Rights Act* 2004' (2005) 26 *Australian Bar Review* 1; JJ Spigelman, 'Principle of Legality and the Clear Statement Principle' (2005) 79 *Australian Law Journal* 769.

3 The term 'common law bill of rights' was, so far as I am aware, first deployed by John Willis in 'Statute Interpretation in a Nutshell' (1938) 16 *Canadian Bar Review* 17. It has been adopted by others: see, eg, DC Pearce and RS Geddes, *Statutory Interpretation in Australia*, (6th edn) LexisNexis Butterworths, Sydney, 2006 at [5.2].

is through what has been described as the 'human rights revolution' of recent decades. This widespread movement represents the resurgence of the philosophy of natural law in common law systems for the first time in three centuries. In England this resurgence is driven, in part, by the influence of civil law, by reason of the subjugation of English law to European law.

Australia's response to this 'revolution' has been a modest one. Nevertheless, the greater salience that has been given to human rights issues by lawyers and judges throughout the world has had, and will continue to have, an influence on the Australian legal system, particularly as the current generation of law students carve their path through that system in the future. Real issues about the proper role of the judiciary in a parliamentary democracy arise in this context. The range of legitimate opinion on this matter is wide and remains the subject of vigorous debate. I do not wish to be understood to take any particular position on the desirability, or otherwise, of a statutory human rights act.

There are now two human rights acts in Australia: in the Australian Capital Territory and Victoria. Such legislation is under consideration in Tasmania and Western Australia, as well as at the Commonwealth level. In New South Wales the introduction of a statutory human rights act was considered and rejected by a Parliamentary Committee, following a rather tentative suggestion by myself.[4] At the moment I do not detect any movement in this position in the New South Wales political debate.

A brief historical perspective is appropriate by reason of the fact that common lawyers have traditionally been reluctant to embrace the rhetoric of rights. It was not always thus.

Blackstone and Bentham

Human rights talk reflects the longstanding tradition of natural law, with which English common lawyers were once very comfortable. That changed about two centuries ago and a new tradition of legal positivism, adopting a command theory of law and a broadly utilitarian philosophy, became the dominant intellectual tradition of English jurisprudence, under the influence of Jeremy Bentham, John Austin and Albert Venn Dicey. The particular target of Bentham's vitriolic attack upon the common lawyers was Sir William Blackstone who, in 1753, delivered the first lectures on English law ever presented at an English university. Until that time Oxford and Cambridge had taught only Roman and canon law.

---

4 See JJ Spigelman, 'Rule of Law – Human Rights Protection' (1999) 18 *Australian Bar Review* 29 at 33; JJ Spigelman, 'Access to Justice and Human Rights Treaties' (2000) 22 *Sydney Law Review* 141 at 149–150; New South Wales, *A New South Wales Bill of Rights: Standing Committee on Law and Justice,* Report No. 17, 2001.

The Inns of Court was the only university for common lawyers.

Blackstone, the first Vinerian Professor of Law at Oxford, presented the first and most influential systematic conspectus of the common law in his *Commentaries*. He had no difficulty about the language of rights. His references to natural law were little more than a ghostly memory of rhetoric past.[5] The quadripartite structure of this seminal work reflected the contemporary terminology of common lawyers. Book 1 is on the rights of persons; Book 2 on the rights of things; Book 3 on private wrongs; and Book 4 on public wrongs. The influence of the legal positivists, in substance, redefined the first two Books. For the last two centuries the common law of England and its epigone, such as the Australian common law, has primarily been a law of wrongs, not balanced by a law of rights.

In the first book of Blackstone's *Commentaries*, 'Of the Rights of Persons', chapter one is entitled 'Of the Absolute Rights of Individuals'. His primary focus was on political or civil rights and, particularly, on the right of property. I would not wish to put Blackstone forward as any kind of model for a contemporary human rights scholar.[6] However,

---

5 See, e.g., David Lieberman, *The Province of Legislation Determined: Legal Theory in Eighteenth-Century Britain*, Cambridge University Press, Cambridge, 1989, ch 1.

6 See, e.g., Albert S Miles et al., 'Blackstone and American Indian Law' (2002) 6 *Newcastle Law Review* 89.

his choice of language must have reflected the practice of the bar at the time.

Of particular significance for the future was the influence of Blackstone's *Commentaries* in the United States of America. In the course of his defence of the American colonists against the conduct of the British executive, Edmund Burke noted that the *Commentaries* had sold as many copies in America as it had in England. Indeed, without any institution such as the Inns of Court, and with a dispersed population, the *Commentaries* became more of a law library than a law book for American legal practice.[7]

Almost a century of American lawyers, from the founding fathers and Chief Justice Marshall down to Abraham Lincoln, learned their law from Blackstone. For that reason, the language of rights particularly – reflected in the Declaration of Rights of Virginia in 1776 and the Bill of Rights adopted in 1791 in the United States Constitution – came naturally to American lawyers. Because of the American Revolution and the adoption of a written constitution, the rights terminology of late eighteenth-century lawyers, when legal

---

7 See Daniel J Boorstin, *The Mysterious Science of the Law: An Essay on Blackstone's Commentaries*, University of Chicago Press, Chicago, 1941; Albert W Alschuler, 'Rediscovering Blackstone' (1996) 145 *University of Pennsylvania Law Review* 1; Paul O Carrese, *The Cloaking of Power: Montesquieu, Blackstone and the Rise of Judicial Activism*, University of Chicago Press, Chicago, 2003, esp pp. 111–112; Albert S Miles, David L Dagley and Christina H Lau, 'Blackstone and his American Legacy' (2001) 5(2) *Australia and New Zealand Journal of Law and Education* 46.

discourse was a dominant feature of politics and society, [8] was frozen in time. In England it gradually disappeared.

Bentham, as a young teenager, was shocked when he attended Blackstone's lectures and heard him support the complexities of the common law. Bentham rejected the theory of natural law. He was a founder of the command theory of law: that all law was an act of will by a sovereign, rather than conforming to some ideal. The arcane mysteries of the common law offended Bentham's monomaniacal pursuit of the principle of utility – the balance of pleasure and pain – as the sole determinant of all proper societal rules. He was the first economic rationalist.

When the French Declaration of Rights appeared, Bentham launched a ferocious attack, declaring:

> Natural rights is simple nonsense: natural and imprescriptible rights, [by which he meant rights which could not be abrogated by a legislature, was] rhetorical nonsense – nonsense upon stilts.

His basic proposition, in common with generations of legal positivists to come, was that rights were created by

---

[8] See, e.g., Douglas Hay, 'Property, Authority and the Criminal Law' in Hay et al., *Albion's Fatal Tree: Crime and Society in Eighteenth Century England*, Pantheon, New York, 1975; 'Introduction' in John Brewer and John Styles (eds), *An Ungovernable People: The English and their Law in the Seventeenth and Eighteenth Centuries*, Hutchinson, London, 1980.

law, rights did not precede government or law. It is not often remembered that the example he used for this proposition, in the 'nonsense on stilts' passage, was the Australian Aborigines, whom he called 'the savages of New South Wales' and who, he said, had no laws and therefore no rights.[9]

From the time of his original 1753 lectures at Oxford, which became the introduction to the *Commentaries*, Blackstone proclaimed that the commencing point of his analysis was the proposition that the purpose of English governance was to promote political and civil liberty. In contrast, Bentham always treated liberty as subordinate to utilitarian reform.[10] Blackstone deployed a dialectical mixture of natural law and legal positivism.

By the middle of the nineteenth century, references to natural law had become distinctly embarrassing to British lawyers. The *Commentaries* was still the basic text, but required updating in numerous respects. Unlike the United States, where new editions of the *Commentaries* continued to be produced and actively deployed in legal discourse, in England an expurgated and updated version emerged. The task was undertaken by Henry John Stephen, whose book *New Commentaries on the Laws of England (Partly Founded on*

---

9 See Jeremy Waldron (ed), *'Nonsense Upon Stilts': Bentham, Burke & Marx on the Rights of Man*, Methuen, London, 1987, p. 53.

10 See Carrese supra, ch 5.

Blackstone) first appeared in 1841. Its numerous subsequent editions and student summaries remained a basic text for the best part of a century. The alterations are revealing.

In his introduction, Blackstone had referred to natural rights and said: 'No human legislature *has power* to abridge or destroy them'. Stephen's *New Commentaries* amended this statement to read: 'No human legislature can *justifiably* abridge or destroy them'. Similarly, the heading of Blackstone's first chapter, which was: 'Of the Absolute Rights of Individuals', had become 'Of Personal Rights'. Assertions such as 'the principal aim of society is to protect individuals in the enjoyment of those absolute rights, which were vested in them by the immutable laws of nature', had disappeared.[11]

None of this is to suggest that the idea of rights played no part in the continuing development of the common law. There can, however, be no doubt that the focus shifted. Rights were no longer regarded as 'natural', in the sense that they had to be treated as existing prior to the creation of a polity and of the laws enacted or developed by custom by the polity. This is what we would today call 'human rights'. Furthermore, the focus remained on civil and political rights, although the original emphasis on property rights

---

11 See Henry John Stephen, *New Commentaries on the Laws of England*, 2nd ed, Butterworths, London, 1848, vol 1 pp. 35, 129; cf William Blackstone, *Commentaries on the Laws of England*, 1st edn, 1965, Book 1, ch 1, p. 120.

waned over the course of the twentieth century until, perhaps, its very end. There was never a focus on the concern of contemporary rights discourse with economic or social rights, or collective rights. Nevertheless, important principles were developed in a manner perfectly consistent with a focus on rights.

Significant areas of the common law, some reinforced by statute, served to protect human rights as they would now be understood. Although the language was somewhat different, the substance was in important respects the same. The central theme of this first lecture is that the protection which the common law affords to the preservation of fundamental rights is, to a very substantial degree, secreted within the law of statutory interpretation.

The law of statutory interpretation has always manifested a dialectic interaction between three approaches, traditionally referred to as the literal rule, the golden rule and the mischief rule. From time to time one or other is given preeminence in accordance with the judicial Zeitgeist. This seems to change every half century or so. The literal rule is now called textualism, the golden rule is now called contextualism and the mischief rule is now called purposive interpretation. In Australia, contextualism and purposivism have come to dominate over recent decades. American jurisprudence, which went through that process long before us, appears to be reverting to textualism. The sources and intensity of threats to fundamental rights are one of the critical elements that may explain these shifts in emphasis.

The *Kisch* case

An excellent example of the way in which the law of statutory interpretation protects fundamental rights is a 1934 judgment of the High Court which, by reason of its vintage, and by reason of the identity of some judges in the majority, does not raise the kinds of difficulties associated with contemporary debates about the judicial role in enforcing human rights.

A great cause célèbre of the mid-1930s was the attempt by the Commonwealth Government to prevent Egon Kisch, a Czech journalist, from attending a Communist front peace congress. Kisch's celebrity has received a recent, moderate revival, particularly at the hands of Justice Hasluck of the Supreme Court of Western Australia.[12] The case affords a good illustration of some issues of statutory interpretation.

Kisch had acquired a degree of intellectual notoriety for his prolific, declamatory, investigative journalism. The

---

12 See Nicholas Hasluck, *Our Man K*, Penguin, Melbourne, 1999; Nicholas Hasluck, 'Waiting for Ulrich: The Kisch and Clinton Cases' (1999) 33 *Quadrant* 28; Nicholas Hasluck, 'Reinventing the Kisch Case' (2000) 2 *University of Notre Dame Australia Law Review* 67; Nicholas Hasluck, *The Legal Labyrinth: The Kisch Case and other Reflections on Law and Literature*, Freshwater Bay Press, Perth, 2003. See also Heidi Zogbaum, *Kisch in Australia: The Untold Story*, Scribe Publications, Melbourne, 2004.

attempt to prevent the Australian public hearing his subversive opinions caused outrage, particularly on the left. A theme of broader appeal was the fear expressed that such conduct could cause right thinking people overseas to think less of Australian intellectual life. Australians never seem so parochial as when we act in fear of being regarded as parochial. Perhaps it was inevitable that Australia's patron saint of the second rate, Norman Lindsay, proclaimed that he and Kisch were both victims of Australian 'suburban complacency'.[13]

Kisch, famously, in an obviously futile attempt to evade those who sought to ban his arrival, first landed in Australia by jumping from his ship in Melbourne – he entitled his subsequent memoir *Australian Landfall.* The leap broke his leg. This, of course, gave him immediate celebrity status. It also enabled him to energise his audiences as he pursued the Soviet policy of 'peace', in the years immediately preceding the Hitler-Stalin pact, with the rallying cry:

> My leg is broken. My English is broken. But my heart is not broken.[14]

---

[13] CMH Clark, *'A History of Australia, VI: The Old Dead Tree and the Young Tree Green (1916–1935)*, Melbourne University Press, Melbourne, 1987, p. 474.

[14] ibid., 471.

The *Immigration Restriction Act* 1901 made provision for a dictation test in a 'European language' of the examiner's choice. Another delegate who sought to address the Peace Congress came from New Zealand. He was given a dictation test in Dutch, failed it and was excluded.[15] Kisch had a reputation as a linguist. Dutch would not do for him. He was given the test in Scottish Gaelic. The issue for determination in the High Court was whether or not Scottish Gaelic was a 'European language'. By majority the High Court held that it was not and, accordingly, the dictation test administered to Kisch was invalid.

Starke J had no doubt about the position. He applied the 'golden rule': give words their grammatical and ordinary meaning, unless the context indicates otherwise. He found no reason to read the words down. Scottish Gaelic was a language used by a large number of people in Scotland. It was a 'European' language. All other members of the Court concluded otherwise.

Rich J noted:

> [T]he provision . . . is dealing with the practical subject of immigration from abroad, particularly from other nations. It ostensibly provides a test against illiteracy and against ignorance of European speech. I think it would be

---

15 ibid., 463.

unreasonable to hold that every distinguishable form of speech which has a home in Europe can be resorted to for the purpose of asking the immigrant to write at dictation a passage of fifty words in length in an European language. The expression 'an European language' means a standard form of speech recognised as the received and ordinary means of communication among the inhabitants in a European community for all the purposes of the social body. Scottish Gaelic is not such a language. Census figures show that it is the speech of a rapidly diminishing number of people dwelling in the remoter highlands of Scotland, and the western islands. It is not the recognised speech of a community organised politically, socially or on any other basis.[16]

Dixon J said:

[T]he substance of the enactment and its subject matter . . . show that the language resorted to is to be taken, ostensibly at least, as a test of fitness of the person to whom the dictation test is administered to take his place in an organised British community.[17]

---

16 *R v. Wilson; Ex parte Kisch* (1934) 52 CLR 234 ('*Kisch*') at 241.

17 ibid., 243.

Dixon J concluded:

> I am very much alive to the difficulty of attaching a definite meaning to these words which will be satisfactory and which will accord with the probable intention of the Legislature. No doubt the Legislature did not itself sufficiently advert to the many uncertainties involved in the expression it used.
>
> . . .
>
> The rules of interpretation require us to take expressions in their context, and to construe them with proper regard to the subject matter with which the instrument deals and the objects it seeks to achieve, so as to arrive at the meaning attached to them by those who use them. To ascertain this meaning the compound expression must be taken and not its disintegrated parts. I am disposed to think that it means here to convey that a test is provided for immigrants depending upon a proper familiarity with some form of speech which in some politically organised European community is regarded as the common means of communication for all purposes.[18]

---

18 ibid., 244.

Evatt J adopted a more international perspective when he concluded:

> It cannot be denied that, in the *Immigration Act* dictation test, the Australian Parliament represented to the Governments and nationals of all other countries that exclusion from Australia would be the result of an elementary dictation test limited to those languages which the Governments of the world would immediately recognise as an accepted or standard language of modern Europe. Scottish Gaelic is not such a language.[19]

The *Kisch* case occurred before the courts decided to have recourse to a wide range of extrinsic materials, including parliamentary debates. Nevertheless it is difficult to believe that the High Court was unaware of the true origins of the dictation tests. The intention of Parliament when enacting the original *Immigration Restriction Act* 1901 was that the dictation test should be applied for the purpose of excluding coloured migrants. It was the core provision of what became known as The White Australia Policy.

The use of a dictation test as a camouflage for a policy of racial exclusion was first introduced in Natal and, at the express suggestion of the British Colonial Secretary Joseph

---

19 ibid., 247.

Chamberlain, was adopted by a number of the Australian colonies.[20] The purpose of this camouflage was to preserve the illusion of an absence of racial discrimination within the British Empire, a matter especially sensitive in India, the Jewel of the Empire. The sensitivity of the imperial centre to any of the white colonies behaving in this manner was exacerbated by the fact that Great Britain was at that time cultivating the newly emerging power in the Far East, Japan, which had shown itself to be particularly sensitive to expressions of racial discrimination, including by the Australian colonies.

When Edmund Barton introduced the *Immigration Restriction Bill* into the first Commonwealth Parliament, he implemented this imperial policy.[21] Amendments were unsuccessfully moved by the Labor Party to expressly exclude non-European migrants. Indeed, a handful of non-European applicants were allowed into Australia by means of the selection of a language under the dictation test in which they proved proficient. The degree of administrative discretion conferred by permitting the examiner to select the language invited abuse, which no doubt occurred.

---

20 See John Quick and Robert Randolph Garran, *The Annotated Constitution of the Australian Commonwealth*, Angus & Robertson, Sydney, 1901, pp. 626–627.

21 See Geoffrey Bolton, *Edmund Barton: The One Man for the Job*, Allen & Unwin, Sydney, 2000, pp. 243–245.

AB Piddington KC, 73 years old but driven by fear of fascism and the emergence of the New Guard, appeared for Kisch in the High Court. In Court, he handed up volume one of the *Australian Encyclopaedia* (1926) drawing their Honours' attention to pp 653 *et seq.*[22] That text made the racist origins of the Act quite clear. It said:

> The first federal parliament . . . set itself to give effect to the popular demand for the exclusion of Asiatics, and after much controversy the language test was agreed upon . . . *It was understood from the first that European immigrants would not be required to pass the test.*[23]

This little bit of extrinsic material was handed up, without comment it appears, from either the bar or the bench. Nonetheless, it was powerful as a guide to the eventual result in *Kisch*. It is a technique of advocacy that the late Sir Maurice Byers QC, a barristers' barrister, used to describe as 'putting the ball in the scrum'.

Piddington made no submission to the High Court that the Parliament intended the dictation test to be administered only to coloured applicants. He made no submission that the

---

22 *Kisch* at 237.

23 Arthur Wilberforce Jose and Herbert James Carter (eds), *The Illustrated Australian Encyclopaedia*, Angus & Robertson, Sydney, 1925, vol 1 pp. 653–654 (emphasis added).

Act was never intended to apply to a white Czech, even if he was a Bolshevik. Piddington did not submit that rather than reading down the words 'European language', it would better accord with the parliamentary intention to read down the word 'person' in the relevant section, to mean 'non-white' person. Perhaps, particularly with a newly aggressive Japan, it was too hard to be frank. More likely, it was the continued sensitivities of the British Empire that prevented anything like that being uttered in public – whether from the bar table or in a judgment.

The first use of the dictation test for a white person, of which I am aware, was in 1914. Miss Ellen Fitzgibbon, a young Irish girl, described as 'of rather attractive appearance' was deported after failing a test in Swedish. The only clue we have is that on her voyage the captain of the ship had occasion to have Miss Fitzgibbon examined by a medical officer.[24] Preserving the public morals was still a factor in the mid-thirties. In 1936, a year after the Kisch affair, the dictation test was used to exclude an English woman, Mrs M Freer, on the ground that her entry might lead to the dissolution of a 'perfectly good Australian marriage'.[25] The power was also frequently used for political purposes.

---

[24] See Gavin Souter, *Lion and Kangaroo: The Rise of a Nation, 1901–1919,* Collins, Sydney, 1978, p. 90.

[25] F K Crowley (ed), *A New History of Australia*, Heinemann, Melbourne, 1974, p. 448.

In the *Kisch* case reference was made to the importance of context. Indeed, it was context that proved determinative. The context on which reliance was placed extended beyond the Act itself to encompass the scope and purpose of the legislation. The emphasis was on the significance of language, in contrast to dialects, in a world-wide system of polities and societies. This was the context adopted by the Court as pertinent to the interpretation of legislation regulating the migration of persons from one polity/society to another polity/society. That is why the word 'language' was identified as having been used with reference to a broader grouping than a distinct minority language or dialect. By these orthodox steps of statutory interpretation, a result affirming the right to freedom of movement was attained.

Principles of interpretation

Statutory interpretation is not merely a collection of maxims or canons. It is a distinct body of law. It is capable of disaggregation, as the basic Australian text does, into categories such as: 'extrinsic aids to interpretation'; 'intrinsic or grammatical aids to interpretation'; and 'legal assumptions'.[26] An American analysis refers to this tripartite classification as: 'referential canons'; 'linguistic canons'; and 'substantive

---

[26] See Pearce and Geddes supra, the Chapter headings of chs 3, 4 and 5.

canons'.[27] Amongst the 'substantive canons' the authors refer to legal presumptions and clear statement rules. In this respect it can be said that the common law developed a bill of rights in recognition of the fact that infringement of rights will often occur by statute or by the exercise of powers under statute.

I use the term 'bill of rights' because it has acquired a level of acceptance by wide usage, and is not yet replaced by 'charter of rights'. Of course, the original 'Bill of Rights' amendments to the United States Constitution, reflected, in large measure, the understanding of what was then referred to as 'the rights of Englishmen'. Blackstone's *Commentaries* were the most influential contemporary exposition of these rights. Many of the principles, then called rights, live on in the law of statutory interpretation. It may be more accurate to refer to a 'common law bill of principles', but that would not convey the sense of a systematic protection of human rights which is the result, as a matter of practical reality, of those aspects of the law of statutory interpretation which constitute common law protections of human rights.

---

27 See William N Eskridge Jr and Philip P Frickey, 'Quasi-Constitutional Law: Clear Statement Rules as Constitutional Lawmaking' (1992) 45 *Vanderbilt Law Review* 593 at 595.

It is an inevitable concomitant of statutory interpretation that it is necessary to invoke interpretative principles which reflect values and assumptions that are so widely held as not to require express repetition in every text. Often these principles will play the determinative role in identifying the meaning of the text. The existence of such background assumptions has been identified in many different circumstances of constitutional and statutory interpretation.[28]

The basic principle that Parliament did not intend to invade fundamental rights, freedoms and immunities has been well established in Australia at least since 1907, when the High Court adopted a passage from a text on statutory interpretation that said:

> It is in the last degree improbable that the legislature would overthrow fundamental principles, infringe rights, or depart from the general system of law, without expressing its intention with irresistible clearness; and to give any such effect to general words, simply because they have that meaning in their widest, or usual, or natural

---

28 See, e.g., John Bell and George Engle, *Cross on Statutory Interpretation*, 3rd edn, Butterworths, London, 1995, pp. 165–166; Cass R Sunstein, 'Interpreting Statutes in the Regulatory State' (1989) 103 *Harvard Law Review* 405; *Australian Communist Party v. Commonwealth* (1951) 83 CLR 1 at 193 (the rule of law); *Egan v. Chadwick* (1999) 46 NSWLR 563 at [16]–[25] (responsible government).

> sense, would be to give them a meaning in which they were not really used.[29]

This principle, also applicable to subordinate legislation,[30] has been expressed and re-expressed by the High Court on numerous occasions.[31] An authoritative statement is in a unanimous joint judgment of the High Court in *Coco v. The Queen*:

> The insistence on express authorization of an abrogation or curtailment of a fundamental right, freedom or immunity must be understood as a requirement for some manifestation or indication that the legislature has not only directed its attention to the question of the abrogation or curtailment of such basic rights, freedoms or immunities but has also determined upon abrogation or curtailment of them. The courts should not impute to the legislature an intention to interfere with fundamental

---

29 *Potter v. Minahan* (1908) 7 CLR 277 ('*Potter*') at 304. The text was the fourth edition of *Maxwell on Interpretation of Statutes* (Sweet & Maxwell, London, 1905). Subsequent editions of that text substitute much wider language to this passage and should be treated with care; see *R v Janceski* (2005) 64 NSWLR 10 ('*Janceski*') at [67]–[88].

30 See *Hill v. Green* (1999) 48 NSWLR 161 at [5]–[10], [143].

31 See, e.g., *Bropho v. Western Australia* (1990) 171 CLR 1 at 18; *Wentworth v. New South Wales Bar Association* (1992) 176 CLR 239 at 252; *Coco v. The Queen* (1994) 179 CLR 427 ('*Coco*') at 437; *Daniels Corporation International Pty Ltd v. Australian Competition and Consumer Commission* (2002) 213 CLR 543 ('*Daniels Corp*') at [11].

> rights. Such an intention must be clearly manifested by unmistakable and unambiguous language. General words will rarely be sufficient for that purpose if they do not specifically deal with the question because, in the context in which they appear, they will often be ambiguous on the aspect of interference with fundamental rights.[32]

What is to be regarded as a 'fundamental right, freedom or immunity' is informed by the history of the common law. One list, not intended to be comprehensive, was identified by McHugh J as entitled to a strong presumption against intrusion, in the following way:

> [A] civil or criminal trial is to be a fair trial, a criminal charge is to be proved beyond reasonable doubt, people are not to be arrested or searched arbitrarily, laws, especially criminal laws, do not operate retrospectively, superior courts have jurisdiction to prevent unauthorised assumptions of jurisdiction by inferior courts and tribunals . . . [33]

The general principle is reflected in numerous specific principles of the law of statutory interpretation which can

---

32 *Coco* at 437.

33 *Malika Holdings Pty Ltd v. Stretton* (2001) 204 CLR 290 ('*Malika Holdings*') at [28].

be set out as a common law bill of rights, based on the presumed intention of Parliament which operates in the absence of a clear indication to the contrary in the statute. These include rebuttable presumptions that the Parliament did not intend to:

- retrospectively change rights and obligations;[34]
- infringe personal liberty;[35]
- interfere with freedom of movement;[36]
- interfere with freedom of speech;[37]
- alter criminal law practices based on the principle of a fair trial;[38]

---

34 See *Cox v. Hakes* (1890) 15 App Cas 506 esp at 519, 528, 534; *Newell v. The King* (1936) 55 CLR 707 at 711; *Maxwell v. Murphy* (1957) 96 CLR 261 at 267; *Fisher v. Hebburn Ltd* (1960) 105 CLR 188 at 194; *Rodway v. The Queen* (1990) 169 CLR 515 at 518; *Esber v. Commonwealth* (1992) 174 CLR 430 at 440–441. The most recent detailed discussion of this principle is Ben Juratowitch, *Retroactivity and the Common Law* (2008) Hart Publishing, Oxford.

35 *R v. Bolton; Ex parte Beane* (1987) 162 CLR 514 at 520, 523, 532; *Al-Kateb v. Godwin* (2004) 219 CLR 562 ('*Al-Kateb*') at [149]–[150]; *Uittenbosch v. Chief Executive, Department of Corrective Services* [2006] 1 Qd R 565 at [7], [12]–[18].

36 *Commonwealth v. Progress Advertising & Press Agency Co Pty Ltd* (1910) 10 CLR 457 at 464; *Potter* at 305–306; *Melbourne Corporation v. Barry* (1922) 31 CLR 174 at 206.

37 *Nationwide News Pty Ltd v. Wills* (1992) 177 CLR 1 at 31; *R v. Secretary of State for the Home Department; Ex parte Simms* [2000] 2 AC 115 ('*Simms*') at 125–127, 130.

38 See, e.g., *Bishop v. Chung Bros* (1907) 4 CLR 1262 at 1273–1274; *Tassell v. Hayes* (1987) 163 CLR 34 at 41; *R v. Fuller* (1994) 34 NSWLR 233 at 237–238; *Thompson v. Mastertouch TV Service Pty Ltd (No 3)* (1978) 38 FLR 397 at 408–409, 412–413; *Environment Protection Authority v. Caltex Refining Co Pty Ltd* (1993) 178 CLR 477 ('*EPA v. Caltex*') at 516–517; *Malika Holdings* at [28].

- restrict access to the courts;[39]
- permit an appeal from an acquittal;[40]
- interfere with the course of justice;[41]
- abrogate legal professional privilege;[42]
- exclude the right to claim self-incrimination;[43]
- extend the scope of a penal statute;[44]
- deny procedural fairness to persons affected by the exercise of public power;[45]
- give executive immunities a wide application;[46]
- interfere with vested property rights;[47]

---

39 *Magrath v. Goldsborough Mort & Co Ltd* (1932) 47 CLR 121 at 134; *Plaintiff S157/2002 v. Commonwealth* (2003) 211 CLR 476 ('*Plaintiff S157*') esp at [30]–[32].

40 *Davern v. Messel* (1984) 155 CLR 21 ('*Davern*') at 30–31, 48, 63, 66.

41 *EPA v. Caltex* at 558.

42 *Corporate Affairs Commission (NSW) v. Yuill* (1991) 172 CLR 319 at 322, 338, 368–369; *Daniels Corp* at [11]. Note also *R (Morgan Grenfell & Co Ltd) v. Special Commissioner of Income Tax* [2003] 1 AC 563 at [7]–[8].

43 *Pyneboard Pty Ltd v. Trade Practices Commission* (1983) 152 CLR 328; *Hamilton v. Oades* (1989) 166 CLR 486 at 495; *Rich v. Australian Securities and Investment Commission* (2004) 220 CLR 129.

44 *Ex parte Fitzgerald; Re Gordon* (1945) 45 SR (NSW) 182 at 186; *Krakouer v. The Queen* (1998) 194 CLR 202 at [62].

45 *Commissioner of Police v. Tanos* (1958) 98 CLR 383 at 395–396; *Annetts v. McCann* (1990) 170 CLR 596 at 598; *Ainsworth v. Criminal Justice Commission* (1992) 175 CLR 564 at 575–576.

46 *Board of Fire Commissioners (NSW) v. Ardouin* (1961) 109 CLR 105 at 116; *Puntoriero v. Water Administration Ministerial Corporation* (1999) 199 CLR 575 at [33]–[37], [59]–[68], [113].

47 *Clissold v. Perry* (1904) 1 CLR 363 at 373; *American Dairy Queen (Qld) Pty Ltd v. Blue Rio Pty Ltd* (1981) 147 CLR 677 at 682–683; *Clunies-Ross v. Commonwealth* (1984) 155 CLR 193 at 199–200.

- authorise the commission of a tort;[48]
- alienate property without compensation;[49]
- disregard common law protection of personal reputation;[50] and
- interfere with equality of religion.[51]

This common law bill of rights overlaps with, but is not identical to, the list of human rights specified in international human rights instruments given legislative force in some jurisdictions. That development will have an influence upon the degree of emphasis to be given to these presumptions. It will also influence the articulation of new presumptions. For example, the legislative proscription of discrimination on the internationally-recognised list of grounds – gender, race, religion, etc. – could well lead to a presumption that Parliament did not intend to legislate with such an effect. I am unaware of any authority which says that, but I can see how this proposition could now be added to the common law bill of rights.

---

48 *Coco* at 435–438.

49 *Commonwealth v. Hazeldell Ltd* (1918) 25 CLR 552 at 563; *Colonial Sugar Refining Co Ltd v. Melbourne Harbour Trust Commissioners* [1927] AC 343 at 359; *Durham Holdings Pty Ltd v. New South Wales* (2001) 205 CLR 399 at [28]–[31].

50 *Balog v. Independent Commission Against Corruption* (1990) 169 CLR 625 at 635–636.

51 *Canterbury Municipal Council v. Moslem Alawy Society Ltd* (1985) 1 NSWLR 525 at 544 per McHugh JA.

I note in this context, that a right not to be subject to racial discrimination was recognised at common law in a case which is not well remembered. In 1943, the West Indian cricket captain, Learie Constantine, was refused service at a prominent London hotel. He successfully sued for damages in an action on the case. The authorities referred to in that judgment are replete with references to common law rights. The judge concluded that Constantine's common law right had been violated.[52] This precedent could have been (but was not) developed into a general right at common law not to be discriminated against on racial grounds. Eventually, legislation established that right.

The right to a fair trial is perhaps the best-established example of a presumption appropriately characterised as part of a common law bill of rights. With the exception of the right to a speedy hearing, which has not been acknowledged in Australia, the Australian law is virtually indistinguishable from the case law with respect to a right of fair trial in those jurisdictions which have adopted a human rights instrument – all of which contain a provision to that effect.[53]

It is not feasible to list exhaustively the attributes of a fair trial. The issue has arisen in a seemingly infinite variety of actual situations in which determining whether something

---

52 *Constantine v. Imperial Hotels Ltd* [1944] 1 KB 693 at 708.

53 See generally JJ Spigelman, 'The Truth Can Cost Too Much: The Principle of a Fair Trial' (2004) 78 *Australian Law Journal* 29.

that was said or done, either before or at the trial, deprived the trial of the quality of fairness to a degree where a miscarriage of justice occurred. There is probably no aspect of preparation for trial or trial procedure which is not touched, indeed often determined, by fair trial considerations. As Lord Devlin once put it:

> [N]early the whole of the English criminal law of procedure and evidence has been made by the exercise of the judges of their power to see what was fair and just was done between prosecutors and accused.[54]

Justice Isaacs said in 1923, with reference to 'the elementary right of every accused person to a fair and impartial trial':

> Every conviction set aside, every new criminal trial ordered, are mere exemplifications of this fundamental principle.[55]

I will not repeat what I have written elsewhere about the scope and range of circumstances in which the principle of a fair trial falls to be applied.[56] It is sufficient for present

---

54 *Connelly v. Director of Public Prosecutions* [1964] AC 1254 at 1347.

55 See *R v. Macfarlane; Ex parte O'Flanagan* (1923) 32 CLR 518 at 541–542.

56 Spigelman, 'The Truth Can Cost too Much: The Principle of a Fair Trial' supra.

purposes to indicate that this is a fundamental common law right and, accordingly, the principle of statutory interpretation with which I am here concerned will be applied, and applied with some strictness. Parliament will need to state, with clarity, that it intends to impinge upon the traditional incidents of the criminal trial which have been developed over the centuries by the application of the principle of a fair trial.

I give one example of this process at work, in three separate Australian jurisdictions over recent years, with respect to the interpretation of provisions giving a general right of appeal. The High Court had long before determined that general words in a provision establishing a right of appeal do not extend to modifying the conclusive effect of a verdict of acquittal, to which the court referred as an 'ancient and universally recognised constitutional right'.[57]

Similarly Deane J said in *Rohde v. Director of Public Prosecutions (Cth)*[58] in the context of appeals by the Crown against sentence:

> A conferral of such a prosecution right of appeal infringes the essential rationale of the traditional common law rule against double jeopardy in the administration of

---

[57] *Wall v. R; Ex parte King Won (No 1)* (1927) 39 CLR 245 at 250; see also *Secretary of State for Home Affairs v. O'Brien* [1923] AC 603 at 610.

[58] (1986) 161 CLR 119 at 128–129.

> criminal justice in a manner comparable to a conferral of a prosecution right of appeal against a trial acquittal . . . As a matter of established principle, a general statutory provision should not ordinarily be construed as conferring or extending such a prosecution right of appeal against sentence unless a specific intention to that effect is manifested by very clear language.

In New South Wales, the Court of Criminal Appeal applied this principle when refusing to allow the Crown to appeal from an interlocutory indication by a trial judge that he intended to direct a verdict of acquittal.[59] Furthermore, when legislation was introduced granting the Crown, in specified circumstances, a right to appeal from an acquittal, the fundamental nature of the principle of the criminal law involved, combined with the principle against retroactivity, meant that the Court held that legislation did not apply to proceedings which had been instituted prior to the statute coming into effect.[60]

In Victoria the issue arose with an attempt by the Crown to appeal an allegedly inadequate penalty imposed for a conviction for contempt. The Victorian Court of Appeal concluded that a generally expressed right of appeal should not be construed as extending to the Crown with

---

59 See *R v. Cheng* (1999) 48 NSWLR 616.

60 See *R v. JS* [2007] NSWCCA 272 esp at [26]–[48].

respect to a sentence imposed following a conviction for contempt.[61]

In Queensland, the Court of Appeal also determined that a broadly stated statutory right of appeal did not apply to an order dismissing a contempt proceeding.[62]

These principles remain of robust utility.

The principle of legality

In recent years this range of presumptions, canons or maxims with substantive content, have been categorised together under the general concept of the 'principle of legality'. This principle was reintroduced into contemporary discourse as a phrase found in the fourth edition of *Halsbury's Laws of England.* There it was employed as equivalent to the traditional phrase 'the rule of law', albeit in a narrower sense to many uses of that concept.[63] It is, however, a concept with a long history and was expounded at some length in the early 1950s by Glanville Williams.[64] He was concerned with the application in the English criminal law of the traditional maxim of *nullum crimen sine lege, nullum poena sine lege* – no

---

61 See *Director of Public Prosecutions v. Garde-Wilson* (2006) 15 VR 640 esp at [15]–[26].

62 See *Henderson v. Taylor* [2007] 2 Qd R 269 esp at [13]–[16], [26]–[27], [73]–[78].

63 See *Halsbury's Laws of England,* 4th ed, reissued, 1996, vol 8(2) at [6].

64 See Glanville Williams, *Criminal Law,* 1st ed, Stevens, London, 1953, pp. 434–465, then ch 12 of this seminal text.

crime or punishment save in accordance with law.[65] This maxim was applied in a number of respects: by the principle against retroactivity; by the rule of strict construction of penal statutes; and by the need for certainty in draftsmanship, which has a long history as an integrative concept.

In the case which established 'the principle of legality' as a unifying principle in English law, Lord Hoffmann said, in a passage subsequently quoted with approval by Gleeson CJ[66] and by Kirby J[67] and, in New Zealand, by Elias CJ and Tipping J:[68]

> [T]he principle of legality means that Parliament must squarely confront what it is doing and accept the political cost. Fundamental rights cannot be overridden by general or ambiguous words. This is because there is too great a risk that the full implications of their unqualified meaning may have passed unnoticed in the democratic process. In the absence of express language or necessary implication to the contrary, the courts therefore presume that even the most general words were intended to be subject to the basic rights of the individual. In this way the courts of the

---

65 See also Aly Mokhtar, 'Nullum Crimen, Nulla Poena Sine Lege: Aspects and Prospects' (2005) 26 *Statute Law Review* 41.

66 *Plaintiff S157* at [30]; *Al-Kateb* at [19].

67 *Daniels Corp* at [106]; *Attorney-General (WA) v. Marquet* (2003) 217 CLR 545 at [180].

68 *R v. Pora* [2001] 2 NZLR 37 at [53].

> United Kingdom, though acknowledging the sovereignty of Parliament, apply principles of constitutionality little different from those which exist in countries where the power of the legislature is expressly limited by a constitutional document.[69]

As Lord Simon of Glaisdale once said, the canons of construction 'are . . . constitutionally salutary in helping to ensure that legislators are not left in doubt as to what they are taking responsibility for'.[70] This idea is the same as that expressed by John Marshall, Chief Justice of the United States, in 1820, when he said of the rule that penal laws are to be construed strictly:

> It is the legislature, not the Court, which is to define the crime and ordain its punishment.[71]

The range of principles of the law of statutory interpretation, to which it is convenient to refer under the unifying concept of the principle of legality, are well

---

69 *Simms* at 131. See also *B v. Director of Public Prosecutions* [2000] 2 AC 428 at 470; *Ngati Apa Ki Te Waipounamu Trust v. R* [2000] 2 NZLR 659 at [82]; *R v. JS* at [36]-[37]; *Lodhi v. R* (2006) 199 FLR 303 at [32]; *Minister for Immigration and Citizenship v. Haneef* [2007] FCAFC 203 at [111]; *Minister for Immigration and Multicultural and Indigenous Affairs v. Al Masri* (2003) 126 FCR 54 at [82]–[85]; *Watkins v. Queensland* [2007] QCA 430 at [64].

70 *Ealing London Borough Council v. Race Relations Board* [1972] AC 342 at 361.

71 *United States v. Wiltberger*, 18 US (5 Wheat) 76 (1820) at 95.

known to every parliamentary drafter: they have been well established for such a long period of time, and have been reaffirmed on many occasions. The courts are entitled to approach statutory interpretation on the assumption that, if the principles are not to be applied, the Parliament will say so, or otherwise express its intention by identifying the results it wishes to achieve in a way that will ensure that the law of statutory interpretation does not interfere with that occurring. As Gleeson CJ has said with respect to this principle:

> The presumption is not merely a common sense guide to what a Parliament in a liberal democracy is likely to have intended; it is a working hypothesis, the existence of which is known both to Parliament and the courts, upon which statutory language will be interpreted. The hypothesis is an aspect of the rule of law.[72]

Ambiguity

There is a tendency in some authorities to give a narrow application to the presumption relevant to the case before the court, on the basis that it is first necessary to find an ambiguity in the statutory formulation before the presumption can operate. In both the House of Lords and the

---

72 *Electrolux Home Products Pty Ltd v. Australian Workers Union* (2004) 221 CLR 309 ('*Electrolux*') at [21].

New Zealand Court of Appeal, such references appear in judgments which emphasise the restrictive operation of common law presumptions in comparison with statutory provisions for interpretation in a human rights act.[73] In my opinion, this reflects an unnecessarily restrictive view of the concept of ambiguity in the law of statutory interpretation. When the relevant common law presumption is understood as a specific application of the principle of legality, it is not appropriate to take a narrow approach to what is meant by ambiguity.

I have, on more than one occasion, had reason to draw on the observations of a master of statutory interpretation, Lord Simon of Glaisdale[74] – both an officer of the Simplified Spelling Society and a scrabble tragic – including the following:

> Words and phrases of the English language have an extraordinary range of meaning. This has been a rich resource in English poetry (which makes fruitful use of the resonances, overtones and ambiguities), but it has a

---

[73] See *R v. Secretary of State to the Home Department: Ex parte Pierson* [1998] AC 539 at 587; *Quilter v. Attorney-General* [1998] 1 NZLR 523, 526, 541–542, 581.

[74] The titles of two earlier addresses were drawn from Lord Simon's judgments: 'Identifying the Linguistic Register' and 'The Poet's Rich Resource': see above n 2. See also his Lordship's series of articles on 'English Idioms from the Law' (1960) 76 *Law Quarterly Review* 283 and 429; (1962) 78 *Law Quarterly Review* 245; and (1965) 81 *Law Quarterly Review* 52.

> concomitant disadvantage in English law (which seeks unambiguous precision, with the aim that every citizen shall know as exactly as possible, where he stands under the law).[75]

Perhaps not without irony, the word 'ambiguity' is itself ambiguous. It is not necessarily limited to situations of lexical or verbal ambiguity and grammatical or syntactical ambiguity. The word ambiguity is often used in the more general sense to indicate any situation in which the scope and applicability of a particular statute is, for whatever reason, doubtful.[76] Save where appearing in some interpretation acts, where the narrow conception may be intended, the common law concept of ambiguity should be understood in this broader sense.

Common law doctrines

The protection of fundamental rights, freedoms and immunities (to use the authoritative formulation from the joint judgment in *Coco*) has sometimes been expressed, in a shorthand way, as the protection of common law rights. That terminology can be misleading if it is used in such a way

---

75 *Stock v. Frank Jones (Tipton) Ltd* [1978] 1 WLR 231 at 236.

76 See the references set out in my earlier addresses in the *Newcastle Law Review* above n 2 at 2; 21 *Australian Bar Review* above n 2 at 231–232; *Repatriation Commission v. Vietnam Veterans' Association of New South Wales Branch Inc* (2000) 48 NSWLR 548 at [116].

as to equate the position of fundamental rights, freedoms and immunities with the old presumption that Parliament did not intend to change the common law. There is a clear distinction between legislation which invades fundamental rights etc. and legislation which alters common law doctrines. As Lord Simon of Glaisdale put it in 1975:

> It is true that there have been pronouncements favouring a presumption in statutory construction against a change in the common law . . . Indeed, the concept has sometimes been put (possibly without advertence) in the form that there is a presumption against change in the law pre-existing the statute which falls for construction. So widely and crudely stated, it is difficult to discern any reason for such a rule – whether constitutional, juridical or pragmatic. We are inclined to think that it may have evolved through a distillation of forensic experience of the way Parliament proceeded at a time when conservatism alternated with a radicalism which had a strong ideological attachment to the common law. However valid this particular aspect of the forensic experience may have been in the past, its force may be questioned in these days of statutory activism . . . Whatever subsisting scope any canon of construction may have, whereby there is a presumption against change of the common law, it is clearly a secondary canon . . . – of assistance to resolve

> any doubt which remains after the application of 'the first and most elementary rule of construction', that statutory language must always be given presumptively the most natural and ordinary meaning which is appropriate in the circumstances. Moreover, even at the stage when it may be invoked to resolve a doubt, any canon of a construction against invasion of the common law may have to compete with other secondary canons. English law has not yet fixed any hierarchy amongst the secondary canons: indeed, which is to have paramountcy in any particular case is likely to depend on all the circumstances of the particular case.[77]

To similar effect, Kirby J has often emphasised the duty to obey legislative texts and the impermissibility of adhering to pre-existing common law doctrine in the face of a statute.[78]

McHugh J, on a number of occasions, stated that the presumption that a statute is not intended to alter or abolish common law rights must now be regarded as weak.[79] His Honour did not expressly distinguish in this respect between the presumption against altering common law

---

77 *Maunsell v. Olins* [1975] AC 373 at 394–395.

78 See, e.g., *Regie National des Usines Renault SA v. Zhang* (2002) 210 CLR 491 at [143]–[147].

79 See *Malika Holdings* at [28]–[30]; *Gifford v. Strang Patrick Stevedoring Pty Ltd* (2003) 214 CLR 269 ('*Gifford*') at [36].

doctrines and the presumption against invading common law rights. His Honour did, however, identify circumstances in which the presumption would operate with some strength, identifying that category as 'fundamental legal principles'[80] or as 'a fundamental right of our legal system'.[81] He distinguished 'fundamental rights' which are 'corollaries of fundamental principles' from 'infringements of rights and departures from the general system of law',[82] and distinguished 'a fundamental right' from a right 'to take or not to take a particular course of action'.[83]

With respect to common law doctrines, his Honour emphasised the weakness of the presumption. He said:

> Courts should not cut down the natural and ordinary meaning of legislation evincing an intention to interfere with these lesser rights by relying on a presumption that the legislature did not intend to interfere with them. Given the frequency with which legislatures now abolish or amend 'ordinary' common law rights, the 'presumption' of non-interference with those rights is inconsistent with modern experience and borders on fiction. If the presumption still exists in such cases, its

80 *Malika Holdings* at [28].
81 *Gifford* at [36].
82 *Malika Holdings* at [28].
83 *Gifford* at [36].

> effect must be so negligible that it can only have weight when all other factors are evenly balanced.[84]

If I may be permitted the sin of self-quotation, in a case in which it was the Crown that relied on the so-called presumption that Parliament did not intend to change the common law, I said:

> The principle of statutory interpretation relied on by the Crown is, in my opinion, now of minimal weight. It reflects an earlier era when judges approached legislation as some kind of foreign intrusion. The scope and frequency of legislative amendment of the common law including the common law of criminal procedure, has over many decades been both wide-ranging and fundamental.[85]

This issue has arisen with respect to the manner in which Parliament has, over recent decades, restricted the law of torts. There is a real issue as to what aspects of tort litigation could ever have invoked the principle that legislation must be interpreted on the assumption that it does not alter the common law. As I have sought to show elsewhere, reliance

---

84 ibid. See also the reference by Gleeson CJ in *Electrolux* at [19] and *Malika Holdings* at [29]–[30].

85 See *Janceski* at [62].

on the tort of negligence as establishing common law 'rights' overlooks the fact that fundamental features of the tort, as we know it, were established by legislation which overturned common law rules restricting liability in tort. This included *Lord Campbell's Act,* which overturned the rule against the recovery of damages for the death of another person; the statutory abolition of the doctrine of common employment, by which an injured worker was denied the right to redress whenever injury resulted from the act of a fellow worker; the removal of the immunity of the Crown; the establishment of liability for nervous shock; and apportionment of legislation overturning the absolute nature of the defence of contributory negligence.[86] It may well be that in many of these respects the common law would have developed in the same way. However, that is not what actually happened. In personal injury litigation many so-called 'common law rights' were created by statute. The relevant distinction was emphasised by Justice McHugh, when he said:

> The right to bring an action for psychiatric injury is an ordinary legal right. It is not a fundamental right of our society or legal system similar to the right to have a fair trial or to have a criminal charge proved beyond

---

86 See JJ Spigelman, 'Negligence: The Last Outpost of the Welfare State' (2002) 76 *Australian Law Journal* 432 at 437–438.

a reasonable doubt. Nor is the presumption against interfering with ordinary common law rights of the same strength as the presumption that laws do not operate retrospectively.[87]

I am aware that the Queensland Court of Appeal has applied the case law which refers to fundamental common law rights to statutory restrictions on the ability to seek damages for gratuitous services.[88] Each statutory scheme must be considered separately when applying these principles.

The judicial role

These interpretive principles are of longstanding. The debate about their deployment by common law judges goes back at least as far as Blackstone and Bentham. In many ways Blackstone's account of statutory interpretation in Book 1 of the *Commentaries*[89] is quite contemporary.

What attracted Bentham's outrage, in this as in other aspects, with the common law method, was the fluidity that is introduced by the use of interpretative principles, particularly those which emphasise the context and purpose of the statutory text and specific principles, e.g. that

---

87 See *Gifford* at [37].

88 See *Grice v. Queensland* [2006] 1 Qd R 222 at [25]-[26]; *Kriz v. King* [2007] 1 Qd R 327 at [18].

89 Blackstone supra at 87–92.

Parliament did not intend an absurd result. Bentham found all of this inconsistent with a rational legal order, which required express codification of everything. He made no allowance for ambiguities, gaps, generalities or the scope of language. He found the flexibility that the common law judges retained nothing short of outrageous.[90]

Notwithstanding the assumption in some continental legal systems that complete precision and comprehensiveness of expression is possible, Bentham's obsessiveness has never been accepted in the common law world. His view that every aspect of law could be written down as a complete body of law, which he called a 'Pannomion', has never been achieved, even in the continental codes.

Many years ago Rupert Cross described Bentham's approach to Blackstone as 'pig headed' and referred to:

> The naïve belief manifested throughout so much of his work that it is possible for the laws of a sophisticated society to be formulated in terms of indisputable comprehensibility.[91]

---

[90] See the analysis in Cass R Sunstein and Adrian Vermeule, 'Interpretation and Institutions' (2003) 101 *Michigan Law Review* 885 esp at 890–897.

[91] Rupert Cross, 'Blackstone v Bentham' (1976) 92 *Law Quarterly Review* 516 at 520–521.

Over the centuries, judges in the common law tradition have found that the task of statutory interpretation is never as simple as Bentham thought. There are a range of circumstances in which the application of a statutory formulation is doubtful:

- when the words used are ambiguous or obscure;
- when deciding whether to read down general words;
- when implications are sought to be drawn from a text;
- when considering whether to depart from the natural and ordinary meaning of words, by adopting a strained construction;
- when deciding whether or not a statutory definition or interpretation section does not apply on the basis of an intention to the contrary;
- when giving qualificatory words an ambulatory operation;
- more controversially, whether words and concepts are to be read into a statute by filling gaps.

In the third lecture I will discuss some of these circumstances in detail.

The process of interpretation pursuant to the principle of legality, or any of its sub-principles, may not differ in essence from that to be conducted pursuant to a statutory requirement to interpret any act or statutory instrument to conform with the list of human rights. I will discuss such provisions in the second lecture.

There are examples in legal history of the judiciary applying interpretative principles as a means of subverting legislative intent. The old rule that penal statutes have to be strictly construed – referred to as the 'rule of lenity' in the United States – was developed to mitigate both the harshness of the death penalty then applicable to minor offences, and concomitant attempts by Parliament to restrict benefit of clergy.[92]

The contemporary controversy about judicial activism, particularly in the context of human rights litigation, raises parallel issues. Subject to any constitutional entrenchment of rights, the judiciary must always remember that the interpretative principles are rebuttable.

It is a corollary of the principle of legality, and a manifestation of what Chief Justice Gleeson has felicitously called judicial legitimacy, that the judiciary do not find

---

[92] See Pearce and Geddes supra at [9.8]; Leon Radzinowicz, *A History of English Criminal Law and its Administration from 1750*, Stevens & Sons, London, 1948, vol 1 pp. 83–88; Lawrence M Solan, 'Law, Language and Lenity' (1998) 40 *William and Mary Law Review* 57; Livingston Hall, 'Strict or Liberal Construction of Penal Statutes' (1935) 48 *Harvard Law Review* 748; John Calvin Jeffries Jr, 'Legality, Vagueness, and the Construction of Penal Statutes' (1985) 71 *Virginia Law Review* 189; Sarah Newland, 'Mercy of Scalia: Statutory Construction and the Rule of Lenity' (1994) 29 *Harvard Civil Rights–Civil Liberties Law Review* 197; Stephen Kloepfer, 'The Status of Strict Construction in Canadian Criminal Law' (1983) 15 *Ottawa Law Review* 553.

ambiguity when there is none and recognise clear and unambiguous language when it is presented to them for interpretation. Of course, from time to time, the results of the application of these interpretative principles will give rise to controversy.

There is a substantive distinction between what can permissibly be called 'interpretation' and defiance of the legislative will. The distinction is not as easy to perceive in practice as it is to state in principle. Nevertheless, it is a fundamental distinction which I will address in the third lecture on genuine and spurious interpretation.

You will permit a touch of nostalgia in conclusion. In the 1930s when the *Kisch* case was decided, respect for the courts was unalloyed. No Commonwealth Minister denounced the High Court for letting this rabblerouser pollute the minds of Australian youth or lead Australian women from the path of virtue. There was no electronic lynchmob on talk-back radio.

The Attorney General, Robert Menzies, of Scottish heritage himself and no doubt sensitive to the status of Scottish Gaelic, quietly paid Kisch's costs and let him go home. When the *Sydney Morning Herald* published articles and letters denouncing the judgment for its failure to recognise Scottish Gaelic as the glorious language it was – the most vituperative written under a pseudonym by Sir Mungo MacCallum, Chancellor of the University of Sydney – the newspaper was prosecuted for contempt. I doubt if that would happen today.

Perhaps Egon Kisch left Australia ruminating on the application of his recent experience to the insights into bureaucratic conduct recently published by his old classmate at the Altstadter Gymnasium in Prague – Franz Kafka. We will never know.

THE APPLICATION OF QUASI-CONSTITUTIONAL LAWS

CHAPTER TWO

THE APPLICATION OF QUASI-CONSTITUTIONAL LAWS

There is a tendency in Australia to identify constitutional law with the exegesis of a specific text. Such an approach does not take into account our inheritance of a Westminster system of government. As a joint judgment of the High Court once pointed out:

> To say of the United Kingdom that it has an 'unwritten constitution' is to identify an amalgam of common law and statute and to contrast it with a written constitution which is rigid rather than fluid. The common law supplies elements of the British constitutional fabric.[1]

---

1 See *Lange v. Australian Broadcasting Corporation* (1997) 189 CLR 520 at 562.

The British Constitution, and to a substantial degree our own, has evolved over the course of the centuries through a process of historical accretion and, sometimes, historical accident. To give only one example, George I and George II spoke no, or little, English. For this reason, and also because of their preoccupation with the affairs of the Electorate of Hanover, they did not, unlike their predecessors, attend Cabinet meetings. By the time George III took the throne, the convention was firmly established, by almost half a century of practice, that the monarch did not attend Cabinet.[2]

Our constitution, like the British constitution, is not contained simply in the document called the *Australian Constitution* and the various documents identified as constitutions of the respective States. There are, as is well-known, critical matters that are the subject only of a constitutional convention. These conventions have developed over long periods of time and continue to adjust to new circumstances in a manner which cannot and does not occur with a written text. Sir Victor Windeyer observed, upon the centenary of responsible government, fifty years ago:

> That the players should be making the rules as the game proceeds may seem strange. Yet this has been the course of much British constitutional history. It may well be

---

2 See FW Maitland, *The Constitutional History of England*, Cambridge University Press, Cambridge, 1908, pp. 395.

> inevitable if the organs of government are not to become atrophied; for definition can produce a *rigor iuris*, only one stage removed from *rigor mortis*.[3]

Constitutional significance should be attributed to a number of common law doctrines and a number of statutes. Both are, of course, theoretically able to be amended by Parliament. Nevertheless, the fundamental nature of some of these laws and principles, and the improbability of modifying legislation, justifies treating such statutes and principles of the common law as part of constitutional law.

Many of the principles of interpretation set out in the first lecture under the heading 'The Common Law Bill of Rights', are of constitutional significance. There are a number of references in the case law to various principles of common law described as constitutional rights, for example: the right of access to the courts;[4] the right to personal liberty by invoking *habeas corpus*;[5] the right to a fair trial;[6]

---

3 WJV Windeyer, 'Responsible Government – Highlights, Sidelights and Reflections' (1957) 42 *Journal and Proceedings of the Royal Australian Historical Society* 257 at 272.

4 See *Bremer Vulkan Schiffbau & Maschinenfabrik v. South India Shipping Corp Ltd* [1981] AC 909 at 977; *R v. Secretary of State for the Home Department; Ex parte Leech* [1994] QB 198 at 198–210; *R v. Lord Chancellor; Ex parte Witham* [1998] QB 575 at 585.

5 *Cox v. Hakes* (1890) 15 App Cas 506 at 528; *Ex parte Walsh and Johnson; Re Yates* (1925) 37 CLR 36 at 91.

6 *The King v. Macfarlane; Ex parte O'Flanagan* (1923) 32 CLR 518 at 541.

the conclusive effect of a criminal acquittal;[7] the principle of open justice.[8] Notwithstanding that legislation can amend these rights, they are of such significance as to justify such characterisation.

Many of the principles characterised under the general rubric of the principle of legality, discussed in my first lecture, are accurately characterised as quasi-constitutional. Each is a rebuttable presumption of Parliamentary intention, but they reflect fundamental assumptions about the relationship between citizen and state. That is why they will not be rebutted without clear parliamentary intent.

There are many statutes which are also entitled to be characterised as quasi-constitutional, such as laws creating integrity institutions which, in my opinion, are of a sufficiently wide-ranging and detailed nature to be classified collectively as an 'integrity branch of government'.[9] Where a jurisdiction adopts a statutory form of a bill of rights, that legislation is also entitled to be characterised as 'quasi-constitutional'.

Four examples of such legislation are of relevance to Australian discourse: the *Bill of Rights Act* 1990 of New Zealand, the *Human Rights Act* 1998 of the United Kingdom,

---

7 *Wall v. The King; Ex parte King Won (No 1)* (1927) 39 CLR 245 at 250.

8 *Scott v. Scott* [1913] AC 417 at 473, 477.

9 See Spigelman, 'The Integrity Branch of Government' (2004) 78 *Australian Law Journal* 724.

the *Human Rights Act* 2004 of the Australian Capital Territory and the *Charter of Human Rights and Responsibilities Act* 2006 of Victoria. Adopting such legislation is also under active consideration in other Australian jurisdictions, albeit not my own.

Nature of the text

One of the most fundamental, and frequently overlooked, principles of interpretation is that it is critical to commence with an understanding of the nature of the document which falls to be interpreted. As Professor Paul Freund once remarked:

> We ought not read the Constitution like a last will and testament lest it become one.[10]

This is similar to Sir Victor Windeyer's concept of a '*rigor iuris*'.

There are numerous authorities which emphasise the different approach required for the interpretation of a constitution. As O'Connor J put it in the first decade of federation:

> it must always be remembered that we are interpreting a *Constitution* broad and general in its terms, intended to

---

[10] See Eugene W Hickok Jr (ed), *The Bill of Rights: Original Meaning and Current Understanding*, University Press of Virginia, Charlottesville, 1991, p. 21.

> apply to the varying conditions which the development of our community must involve.[11]

The Privy Council quoted with approval the observation of a Canadian constitutional law scholar:

> The Privy Council, indeed, has laid down that courts of law must treat the provisions of the British North America Act by the same methods of construction and exposition which they apply to other statutes. But there are statutes and statutes; and the strict construction being proper in the case, for example, of a penal or taxing statute or one passed to regulate the affairs of an English parish, would be often subversive of Parliament's real intent if applied to an Act passed to ensure the peace, order and good government of a British colony.[12]

Plainly, a formal constitution, whether or not it incorporates an express bill of rights, is entitled to a distinctively different approach than that appropriate to other forms of legislation. As the Privy Council once said with respect to

---

11 *Jumbunna Coal Mine NL v. Victorian Coal Miners' Association* (1908) 6 CLR 309 at 367–368.

12 *British Coal Corporation v. The King* [1935] AC 500 at 518–519. See also *Edwards v. Attorney-General for Canada* [1930] AC 124 at 136.

the Constitution of Bermuda, which did incorporate a bill of rights:

> It is . . . drafted in a broad and ample style which lays down principles of width and generality . . . [and which] calls for a generous interpretation avoiding what has been called 'the austerity of tabulated legalism', suitable to give individuals the full measure of fundamental rights and freedoms referred to.[13]

The difficulties that may be occasioned in the task of interpreting a constitutional bill of rights, is illustrated by the narrow five to four majority of the Privy Council that upheld the validity of the mandatory death penalty in some Caribbean nations.[14]

Lord Hoffmann, writing for the majority which upheld the full effect of the statute conferring a mandatory death penalty, noted at [28]:

> Parts of the Constitution, and in particular the fundamental rights provision in Chapter III, are expressed in general and abstract terms which invite the participation of the judiciary in giving them sufficient flesh to answer concrete

13 *Minister of Home Affairs v. Fisher* [1980] AC 319 at 328. See also *Attorney-General (Trinidad and Tobago) v. Whiteman* [1991] 2 AC 240 at 247.

14 *Boyce v. The Queen* [2005] 1 AC 400.

> questions . . . The text is a 'living instrument' when the terms in which it is expressed, in their constitutional context, invite and require periodic examination.

His Lordship indicated a clear limit to the living instrument approach when he said at [29]: 'the Constitution does not confer upon the judges a vague and general power to modernise it'.

He concluded:

> [59] The 'living instrument' principle has its reasons, its logic and its limitations. It is not a magic ingredient which can be stirred into a jurisprudential pot together with 'international obligations', 'generous construction' and other such phrases, sprinkled with a cherished aphorism or two and brewed into a potion which will make the Constitution mean something which it obviously does not. If that provokes accusations of literalism, originalism and similar heresies, their Lordships must bear them as best they can.

The dissentients, led by Lord Bingham, were equally forthright, saying that the majority judgment:

> [78] . . . puts a narrow and over-literal construction on the words used, gives little or no weight to the principles

> which should guide the approach to interpretation of constitutional provisions, gives little or no weight to the human rights guarantees which the people of Barbados intended to embed in their constitution and puts Barbados in flagrant breach of its international obligations.[15]

The debate as to the proper approach to constitutional interpretation is not directly relevant to the matters I am now considering, namely, the common law principles of statutory interpretation that I have grouped as a 'common law bill of rights' and the statutory human rights acts. Nevertheless, some aspects of constitutional interpretation may have an analogous application for the interpretation of quasi-constitutional laws. There is some similarity in the approaches that have been adopted between constitutional and quasi-constitutional texts.

In this lecture, I wish to focus on the close analogy between the rules for interpretation contained in the common law bill of rights, and the special provisions requiring courts to strive to interpret other legislation to be compliant with human rights. The approach to these matters reflects the quasi-constitutional nature of the two lists of rights.

---

15 See also *Matthew v. Trinidad and Tobago* [2005] 1 AC 433 at [42]–[46], [56]–[58].

Rights-compliant interpretation

The law of statutory interpretation has become the most important single aspect of legal practice. Significant areas of the law are determined entirely by statute. No area of the law has escaped statutory modification. It is, perhaps, a little ironic that one of the areas of the law least affected by statutory modification is, in fact, the law of statutory interpretation. As a matter of appearance, the introduction into interpretation acts of a requirement for purposive interpretation was substantive. However, by the time that legislation was introduced such an approach had been adopted by the judiciary and replaced the former literalist approach.

The most significant statutory change to the law of statutory interpretation is the introduction of the special interpretation provisions in human rights acts, which impose an obligation upon courts to interpret *other* legislation so as to be consistent with the rights set out in the human rights act. Those rights can be more extensive, or less extensive, than the common law bill of rights which I discussed in my first lecture. There is, however, a substantial overlap. The rights-compliant interpretation provisions are potentially of constitutional significance. Their application raises some fundamental issues about the nature of the interpretative process and the relationship between the judiciary and the Parliament.

There are four rights-compliant interpretation provisions relevant for our purposes. The first is s 6 of the *New Zealand Bill of Rights Act* 1990 which provides:

> Wherever an enactment can be given a meaning that is consistent with the rights and freedoms contained in this Bill of Rights, that meaning shall be preferred to any other meaning.

The second such provision is s 3 of the *Human Rights Act* 1998 of the United Kingdom which provides:

> 3(1) So far as it is possible to do so, primary legislation and subordinate legislation must be read and given effect in a way which is compatible with the Convention rights.

The first such act passed in Australia was the *Human Rights Act* 2004 (ACT) which, in its original form, provided:

> 30(1) In working out the meaning of a Territory law, an interpretation that is consistent with human rights is as far as possible to be preferred.
>
> (2) Subsection (1) is subject to the *Legislation Act*, section 139.

Section 139 of the *Legislation Act* is the common provision of Australian interpretation acts requiring the interpretation that would best achieve the purpose of the law to be preferred to any other interpretation.

In Victoria, the *Charter of Human Rights and Responsibilities Act* provides:

> 32(1) So far as it is possible to do so consistently with their purpose, all statutory provisions must be interpreted in a way that is compatible with human rights.

The legislative history of the ACT *Human Rights Act* is pertinent. The ACT Act was based on a report prepared by the ACT Bill of Rights Consultative Committee which recommended wording based on the New Zealand and United Kingdom approaches as follows:

> A court or tribunal must interpret a law of the Territory to be compatible with human rights and must ensure that the law is given effect to in a way that is compatible with human rights, as far as it is possible to do so.[16]

---

[16] See ACT Bill of Rights Consultative Committee, *Towards an ACT Human Rights Act,* 2003, at Appendix 4: *Human Rights Bill* 2003, ACT, cl 3; Hilary Charlesworth, 'Human Rights and Statutory Interpretation' in Suzanne Corcoran and Stephen Bottomley (eds), *Interpreting Statutes*, Federation Press, Sydney, 2005, p. 114; Hilary Charlesworth, 'Australia's First Bill of Rights: The Australian Capital Territory's Human Rights Act' in Tom Campbell, Jeffrey Goldsworthy and Adrienne Stone (eds), *Protecting Rights without a Bill of Rights: Institutional Performance & Reform in Australia*, Ashgate, Aldershot, 2006, pp. 293–294.

The recommendation was not adopted. By reason of the express provision making s 30 subject to the purposive test, Professor Hilary Charlesworth observed:

> At first sight, then, s 30 appears to make a human rights interpretation of legislation available only when it is clear that the Legislative Assembly did not intend otherwise. In this sense it could be read as a codification of the 'principle of legality' by which Parliament is assumed not to intend to impinge on basic rights unless it uses clear words to do so. This may suggest that s 30 is weaker than both its New Zealand and United Kingdom counterparts in promoting a human rights dialogue.[17]

When the rights-compliant interpretation provision is made expressly subject to the purposive requirement, its operation would probably be very similar to the principle of legality. Nevertheless, it can have some additional force when there is doubt about Parliament's intention in other legislation because it is more likely that the judiciary will apply an express parliamentary authority than a common law principle.

---

17 See Charlesworth, 'Human Rights and Statutory Interpretation' supra at 115; Charlesworth, 'Australia's First Bill of Rights' supra at 295.

Following a review of the *Human Rights Act* it was recommended that:

> Section 30 should be amended to clarify that a human rights consistent interpretation must prevail unless this would defeat the purpose of the legislation.[18]

Subsequently, a bill has been passed which, *inter alia*, amends s 30, so that it is almost identical to the Victorian Act, to provide:

> So far as it is possible to do so consistently with its purpose, a Territory law must be interpreted in a way that is compatible with human rights.

> This change will come into effect on 1 January 2009. The Explanatory Memorandum for the Bill explained:

> It clarifies the interaction between the interpretative rule and the purposive rule such that as far as it is possible a human rights consistent interpretation has to be taken to all provisions in Territory laws. This means that unless the law is intended to operate in a way that is inconsistent with the right in question, the interpretation

---

18 See ACT Department of Justice and Community Safety, *Human Rights Act 2004: Twelve-Month Review – Report*, 2006, Recommendation 5 at 33.

> that is most consistent with human rights must prevail. This is consistent with the Victorian approach contained in subsection 32(1) of the *Charter of Human Rights and Responsibilities Act* 2006. It also draws on jurisprudence from the United Kingdom such as the case of *Ghaidan v Godin-Mendoza* [2004] 2 AC 557 cited recently by the ACT Supreme Court in *Kingsley's Chicken Pty Limited v Queensland Investment Corporation and Canberra Centre Investments Pty Limited* [2006] ACTCA 9.

As I will endeavour to show, *Ghaidan* is an inappropriate source of guidance and its citation by the ACT Supreme Court did not suggest its adoption.

The courts that must apply the interpretation provisions of the ACT and Victorian Acts will draw upon the New Zealand and United Kingdom case law. There are, however, differences in the legislative formulations which may be of significance.

The Victorian and ACT Acts, unlike both the New Zealand and United Kingdom provisions, make reference to the purpose of the legislation. In the Victorian and recently amended ACT formulation there is a reference to 'consistently with their purpose', which focuses attention on matters that are not expressly referred to in either the United Kingdom or New Zealand sections.

Furthermore, the Victorian and ACT Acts adopt, albeit with more explicit guidance, s 5 of the New Zealand Act, which refers to subjecting rights and freedoms to 'reasonable limits'. This is a consideration which distinguishes New Zealand from English case law on the rights-compliant provision.

One of the issues that will arise with respect to the interpretation sections in Victoria and the ACT is what, if any, impact they will have on the interpretation of national uniform legislation. For example, in 2004 and 2005 the Commonwealth and all states and territories enacted interlocking anti-terrorism legislation.

No doubt on the basis of constitutional law advice, the Commonwealth scheme for preventative detention orders was limited to detention for 48 hours, whereas the NSW scheme extended to 14 days. So fine are the distinctions required by the contemporary Chapter 3 jurisprudence of the High Court.

This integrated national scheme which permits detention and questioning warrants, control orders, preventative detention orders, covert search warrants and prohibited contact orders, raises important issues affecting personal liberty. Although there are differences amongst the State Acts, litigation could well invoke the special interpretation sections available only in Victoria and the ACT.

Resolution of this issue could turn on the fact that the current ACT provision is expressly made subject to the purposive test and the Victorian and new ACT provisions refer to 'consistency' with purpose. In each case it is arguable that a nationally uniform regime, interconnecting with Commonwealth legislation for constitutional reasons, was part of the 'purpose'.

Committing yet again the sin of self-quotation, I once observed:

> The *Commonwealth Places (Administration of Laws) Act* is part of a national collaborative scheme between the Commonwealth and all the States. The proposition that one State has impliedly repealed one of the provisions of this scheme without consultation, lacks even a scintilla of force. There is a strong presumption that a legislature in a federal system would not alter a statute that forms part of a collaborative and uniform national scheme, save in express terms. There is nothing express here.[19]

Such an issue has already arisen, without being resolved, in the ACT.[20] Such a situation calls for strong clear statement of principle. There is no room for implied repeal.[21] For analogous reasons, that also appears to be the situation with respect to the binding effect of legislation in the UK adopting the

19 *R v. Porter* (2001) 53 NSWLR 354 at [59].

20 *Capital Property Projects (ACT) Pty Ltd v. Planning and Land Authority* (2006) 152 LGERA 132 at [23].

21 I doubt if *McCawley v. The King* [1920] AC 691; (1920) 28 CLR 106 would be decided the same way today.

European Economic Community treaty and the *European Convention on Human Rights.* This result is a manifestation of the quasi-constitutional character of such legislation.[22]

English authority

The critical issue that arises in the application of rights-compliant interpretation provisions is how far a court can go in modifying the application of the statute and still be undertaking a task that can correctly be identified as one of 'interpretation'. The existing state of English authority suggests that the law in England in this, as in many other respects, has gone further than we have gone and, perhaps, further than we will ever go.

When it comes to applying and interpreting the Charter of Rights of the Australian model and determining what, if any, reliance is to be placed on English authority, the quite different constitutional background must be borne in mind. In significant respects the United Kingdom has surrendered aspects of its sovereignty to the institutions of the European Union. Relevantly, this includes the *European Convention on Human Rights,* which is administered in part by a supranational institution.

Prior to the adoption of the *Human Rights Act* in 1998, England was the most frequent defendant in the European

---

[22] See, e.g., *Thoburn v. Sunderland City Council* [2003] QB 151.

Court of Human Rights at Strasbourg. Indeed, generally, it was an unsuccessful defendant. What happened in such litigation was that the State was sued for failing to comply with its Convention obligations. This even extended at one stage to an action for personal injury which had been unsuccessful in England by reason of a particular rule of the law of tort, which the European Court found constituted a failure to implement Article 6 of the *European Convention on Human Rights* providing for a right to a fair and public hearing. Eventually, the European Court backed off this particular interpretation.[23]

Nevertheless, the success of litigants in the European Court meant that it was the government of England that bore the burden of compensation for its failure to implement a remedy in accordance with Convention rights, rather than some English citizen or corporation that had actually done whatever was being complained about. It was the success of a continuing stream of cases in the European Court of Human Rights that served as an important part of the political stimulus to pass legislation implementing the Convention – 'bringing rights home' it was said – so that it would be English courts that determined matters of this character.

---

23 See JJ Spigelman, 'Access to Justice and Human Rights Treaties' (2000) 22 *Sydney Law Review* 141.

Significantly, as British judges are well aware, a disappointed litigant in England can still take proceedings in Strasbourg. The House of Lords operates in a system where it can be held to be wrong by higher authority, whose case law it is required by statute to take into account.

Specifically, the formulation of the UK rights-compliant interpretation provision was influenced by European Court of Justice judgments on the obligation imposed upon national courts by the European Economic Community treaty.[24] For an Australian audience it is necessary to state that the European Court of Justice is a different body to the European Court of Human Rights.

This background is distinctly different from anything that has been operative in the Australian debate about enacting a statutory Charter of Rights.

At first the rights-compliant interpretation provision in s 3 of the UK *Human Rights Act* was characterised as an enactment of the common law principle of legality.[25]

---

24 See *Ghaidan v. Godin-Mendoza* [2004] 2 AC 557 at [45] ('*Ghaidan*'); *R (IDT Card Services Ireland Ltd) v. IDT Customs & Excise Commissioners* [2006] EWCA Civ 29 at [75]; Francis Bennion, *Statutory Interpretation: A Code*, 4th edn, Butterworths, London, 2002, Section 410 and Francis Bennion, *Supplement to the Fourth Edition of Statutory Interpretation: A Code*, LexisNexis Butterworths, London, 2005, p. 560. See also Geoffrey Lindell, 'The Statutory Protection of Rights and Parliamentary Sovereignty: Guidance from the United Kingdom?' (2006) 17 *Public Law Review* 188.

25 See *R v. Secretary of State for the Home Department; Ex parte Simms* [2000] 2 AC 115 at 131–132 per Lord Hoffmann.

Subsequently, two approaches to the deployment of s 3 emerged, referred to as the cautious approach and the radical approach.[26]

The differences arose clearly in a case in which a rape shield law, which restricted cross-examination of a rape victim, was said to be incompatible with the Convention right to a fair trial. The radical approach to s 3 concluded that it was permissible as a form of interpretation, to construe a section which permitted evidence about sexual behaviour by the complainant, by leave in precisely identified circumstances, an overriding requirement to permit cross-examination if it was 'so relevant to the issue of consent that to exclude it would endanger the fairness of the trial'. The cautious approach rejected this as impermissible, on the basis that '[t]he rule is only a rule of interpretation. It does not entitle the judges to act as legislators'.[27]

---

26 The divergence is reflected in the contrast between Lord Steyn and Lord Hope who, respectively, adopted the radical and cautious approaches in *R v. A (No 2)* [2002] 1 AC 45 ('*R v. A*') at [44] and [108]; see also Daniel Greenberg (ed), *Craies on Legislation*, 8th edn, Sweet & Maxwell, London, 2004, ch 25; Francesca Klug, 'United Kingdom Experience' in Christine Debono and Tanya Colwell (eds), *Comparative Perspectives on Human Rights*, National Institute of Social Science and Law, 2004, p. 5; David Bonner, Helen Fenwick and Sonia Harris-Short, 'Judicial Approaches to the Human Rights Act' (2003) 52 *International and Comparative Law Quarterly* 549 at 555–557.

27 *R v. A* at [108] per Lord Hope; see also at [44] per Lord Steyn.

Eventually the House of Lords adopted the radical approach in *Ghaidan*, which was explained in *Sheldrake*[28] by Lord Bingham as follows:

> [28] . . . First, the interpretative obligation under s 3 is a very strong and far reaching one, and may require the court to depart from the legislative intention of Parliament. Secondly, a convention-compliant interpretation under s 3 is the primary remedial measure and a declaration of incompatibility under s 4 an exceptional course. Thirdly, it is to be noted that during the passage of the Bill through Parliament the promoters of the Bill told both Houses that it was envisaged that the need for a declaration of incompatibility would rarely arise. Fourthly, there is a limit beyond which a convention-compliant interpretation is not possible . . . In explaining why a convention-compliant interpretation may not be possible, members of the committee used differing expressions: such an interpretation would be incompatible with the underlying thrust of the legislation, or would not go with the grain of it, or would call for legislative deliberation, or would change the substance of a provision completely, or would remove its pith and substance, or would violate a cardinal principle of the

---

28 *Ghaidan; Sheldrake v. Director of Public Prosecutions, Attorney-General's Reference (No 4 of 2002)* [2005] 1 AC 264 ('*Sheldrake*').

> legislation (see *Ghaidan* . . . at [33], [49], [110]–[113], [116]). All of these expressions, as I respectfully think, yield valuable insights, but none of them should be allowed to supplant the simple test enacted in the Act: 'So far as it is possible to do so . . .'. While the House declined to try to formulate precise rules (at [50]), it was thought that cases in which s 3 could not be used would in practice be fairly easy to identify.

The first matter to which his Lordship referred is perhaps the most striking to an Australian lawyer. The proposition that a court can interpret a particular act other than in accordance with the intention of Parliament at the time of the enactment of that act is a fundamental change. This conclusion arose from the interpretation of the meaning of the word 'possible' in s 3 in the context of 'reading and giving effect to' other legislation in a manner compatible with the Convention rights 'so far as it is possible to do so'. As Lord Steyn put it:

> This is the intention of Parliament, expressed in s 3, and the courts must give effect to this intention.[29]

In *Ghaidan*, Lord Nicholls said that the word 'possible' is itself ambiguous and posed that the issue was by

---

29 *Ghaidan* at [26].

what standard or criterion 'possibility' is to be judged. His Lordship went on to say:

> [30] . . . [T]he interpretative obligation decreed by s 3 is of an unusual and far-reaching character. Section 3 may require a court to depart from the unambiguous meaning the legislation would otherwise bear. In the ordinary course the interpretation of legislation involves seeking the intention reasonably to be attributed to Parliament in using the language in question. Section 3 may require the court to depart from this legislative intention, that is, depart from the intention of the Parliament which enacted the legislation. The question of difficulty is how far, and in what circumstances, s 3 requires a court to depart from the intention of the enacting Parliament. The answer to this question depends upon the intention reasonably to be attributed to Parliament in enacting s 3.
>
> [31] . . . Since section 3 relates to the 'interpretation' of legislation, it is natural to focus attention initially on the language used in the legislative provision being considered. But once it is accepted that s 3 may require legislation to bear a meaning which departs from the unambiguous meaning the legislation would otherwise bear, it becomes impossible to suppose Parliament intended that the operation of s 3 should depend critically

> upon the particular form of words adopted by the parliamentary draftsman in the statutory provision under consideration. That would make the application of s 3 something of a semantic lottery. If the draftsman chose to express the concept being enacted in one form of words, s 3 would be available to achieve convention-compliance. If he chose a different form of words, s 3 would be impotent.
>
> [32] . . . [T]he intention of Parliament in enacting s 3 was that, to an extent bounded only by what is 'possible', a court can modify the meaning, and hence the effect, of primary and secondary legislation.[30]

The House of Lords purports to accept the traditional judicial role in interpretation, being the implementation of the intention of Parliament. The critical step is, however, that the intention of Parliament expressed in s 3 of the *Human Rights Act* is applied to override the intention of Parliament at the time that the other legislation, including subsequent legislation, is enacted. This is a substantial change in the relationship between Parliament and the judiciary. In substance it constitutionalises the *Human Rights Act*. Such a step had been taken earlier in the course of giving overriding effect to laws of the European

---

30 *Ghaidan* at [28]–[32].

Community, which are quite different from the *European Convention on Human Rights* and are adjudicated upon by a different European court.[31]

The degree to which Parliament's intention in the non-compliant legislation can be overridden is manifest in *Sheldrake.* In the context of the anti-terrorism legislation thereunder consideration, Parliament had expressly listed provisions which imposed only an evidential burden, rather than a burden of proof. The section in issue was not on that list. The House of Lords held, expressly, that it was *not* the intention of Parliament that only an evidential burden be imposed. However, the court concluded that s 3 enabled the court to so find.[32]

More recently, the House of Lords invoked s 3 to qualify the statutory provision for control orders under the *Prevention of Terrorism Act* 2005. Under this scheme the relevant Minister may be permitted by the Court not to disclose material to the subject of an order where the court 'considers that the disclosure would be contrary to the public interest'. The House of Lords held that this provision '. . . should be read and given effect "except where to do so would be incompatible with the right of the controlled person to a fair trial" '.[33]

---

31 See Lindell supra at 24.

32 *Sheldrake* at [5] and [53].

33 *Secretary of State for the Home Department v. MB* [2007] 3 WLR 681 at [72].

Lord Bingham expressed doubt about the course taken because of the mandatory language in the Act.[34] This kind of implied term, importing the words of Article 6 of the Convention in its entirety, had earlier been described by Lord Hoffmann as 'bold' – probably in the 'Yes Minister' sense.[35]

Reading into the Act a qualification expressed in the terms of the protected right is difficult to distinguish from a legislative amendment. When reading English case law in the future, it will be necessary to bear in mind just how different their approach has become. As the authors of a leading text on the *Human Rights Act* have put it:

> The process of interpretation is no longer dominated by a search for the intention of Parliament. Instead the courts' first duty is to adopt any possible construction which is compatible with Convention rights.[36]

In the third lecture, I will discuss how far the English approach can be said to be consistent with the concept of 'interpretation' or, to use the English language, the concept of 'reading and giving effect'. I am, however, sceptical that

---

34 ibid., [44].

35 *R (Hammond) v. Secretary of State for the Home Department* [2005] 3 WLR 1229.

36 Ben Emmerson, Andrew Ashworth and Alison Macdonald, *Human Rights and Criminal Justice*, 2nd edn, Sweet & Maxwell, London, 2007, [3–59].

Australian judges will go as far as the English judges have gone. The New Zealanders have not.

New Zealand authority

The New Zealand judiciary has, in some respects, adopted a robust approach with respect to the *Bill of Rights Act* 1990. In *Baigent's* case, the Court of Appeal created a public law remedy by awarding damages against the Crown for breach of the *Bill of Rights Act*.[37] In *Moonen* the Court of Appeal decided that it would, in an appropriate case, declare that a statute unjustifiably impinges on human rights even though the New Zealand Act, unlike the United Kingdom Act, makes no express provision for any such declaration of incompatibility.[38] Chief Justice Elias has indicated that this approach reflects a recognition that there is a hierarchy of statutes, and manifests a process of dialogue between Parliament and the courts.[39]

Notwithstanding this jurisprudence, the New Zealand courts have not adopted the radical approach of the House of Lords to the rights-compliant interpretation provision in the New Zealand Act.[40]

---

37 *Simpson v. Attorney-General (Baigent's case)* [1994] 3 NZLR 667.

38 *Moonen v. Film and Literature Board of Review* [2000] 2 NZLR 9.

39 See Sian Elias, 'Sovereignty in the 21st Century: Another Spin on the Merry-Go-Round' (2003) 14 *Public Law Review* 148 at 157–162.

40 See J F Burrows, *Statute Law in New Zealand*, LexisNexis, Wellington, 2003, esp pp. 242–252; JJ Spigelman, 'Blackstone, Burke, Bentham and the *Human Rights Act* 2004' (2005) 26 *Australian Bar Review* at 8–10.

An example of the difference in approach is found in cases construing statutory provisions which shift the burden of proof. The House of Lords had no difficulty in deploying s 3 of the United Kingdom Act to that effect.[41] In contrast, the New Zealand Court of Appeal did not apply s 6 of the New Zealand Act in that way.[42] Even at common law, in my opinion, the clear statement principle would apply and such a section would often be interpreted to shift only an evidential burden, not the burden of proof.[43]

The same issue came before the recently-established Supreme Court of New Zealand, which upheld the approach of the earlier judgment that interpreted the formulation 'until the contrary is proved' as shifting a burden of proof.[44] The case contained five separate judgments and there are significant differences between them. A majority of three, Justices Blanchard, Tipping and McGrath, with a strong dissent from Chief Justice Elias, affirmed an approach to the New Zealand interpretation clause which is distinctively different from that which has found favour with the English courts.

---

41 *R v. Lambert* [2002] 2 AC 545 at 563, 574–575, 590, 610; see also *R v. Keogh* [2007] 1 WLR 1500.

42 *R v. Phillips* [1991] 3 NZLR 175 at 176–177.

43 Spigelman, 'Blackstone, Burke, Bentham and the *Human Rights Act* 2004' supra at 8.

44 See *R v. Hansen* [2007] 3 NZLR 1 ('*Hansen*').

Before the passage of the United Kingdom *Human Rights Act*, the New Zealand Court of Appeal had interpreted the words 'can be given' in s 6 to mean 'can reasonably be given'.[45]

In a judgment in the House of Lords, Lord Steyn has said:

> The draftsman of the 1998 Act had before him the slightly weaker model in s 6 of the New Zealand *Bill of Rights Act* 1990 but preferred stronger language. Parliament specifically rejected the legislative model of requiring a reasonable interpretation.[46]

His Lordship was referring to Parliament expressly rejecting such a requirement. An amendment requiring any interpretation under the UK Act to be a 'reasonable' interpretation was moved in the UK Parliament and rejected.

The Supreme Court of New Zealand in *Hansen* expressly affirmed the test of 'reasonably possible' interpretation.[47] This may, in part, be explicable by differences in wording, notably the use of the word 'possible' in the UK Act, with the emphatic addition of 'so far as' and 'must be read',

---

45 See *Ministry of Transport v. Noort* [1992] 3 NZLR 260 at 272.

46 *R v. A* at [44]. In my article, 'Blackstone, Burke, Bentham and the *Human Rights Act* 2004' supra at 10, I incorrectly combined the two propositions in Lord Steyn's statement. I had the impression that he suggested that the New Zealand Act imposed a requirement of a reasonableness. However, that occurred by reason of judicial interpretation.

47 At 157–158, 289–290.

compared to the somewhat weaker formulation in the New Zealand Act of 'can be given'. The ACT and Victorian provisions appear to be analogous to the UK provision in this respect. Furthermore, the New Zealand Act also contains in s 4 an express preservation of the doctrine of implied repeal.[48]

An important matter is the interrelationship between s 6, the interpretation provision of the New Zealand Act, and s 5 of that Act, which provides:

> 5 Subject to section 4 of this Bill of Rights, the rights and freedoms contained in this Bill of Rights may be subject only to such reasonable limits prescribed by law as can be demonstrably justified in a free and democratic society.

The majority in *Hansen*, over Elias CJ's dissent, established that the interpretive provision requires the prior application of s 5. That means that if the Court concludes that the apparent inconsistency was justifiable as a 'reasonable limit'

---

48 When the *Human Rights Bill* was debated in the House of Lords, Lord Simon of Glaisdale suggested an amendment to refer to the doctrine of implied repeal. This was done to ensure that *prior* inconsistent legislation would in fact be taken as overruled without the need for a declaration of incompatibility. That the *Human Rights Act* itself should be insulated from subsequent implied repeal was not the focus of attention: see Great Britain, Parliamentary Debates (Hansard), House of Lords, 18 November 1997 at 509–510, 518–529; 19 January 1998 at 1289–1295.

under s 5, the requirement for a rights-compliant interpretation is not engaged. The process of interpretation required a sequence of steps in which the court should first determine whether any inconsistency with a relevant right or freedom is justified. If so, then Parliament's intended meaning would prevail.[49]

Section 5 of the New Zealand Act has no equivalent in the UK Act. It has, however, been adopted in s 28 of the ACT Act and s 7 of the Victorian Act, albeit with specification of a list of relevant factors. It will be necessary for Australian courts to consider whether to follow the New Zealand case law to the effect that these provisions operate anterior to the rights-compliant interpretation provision.

ACT authority

I am unaware of any application of the interpretative provision in the Victorian *Charter*, which only came into force on 1 January this year. There have been a number of cases in the Australian Capital Territory.

The current ACT provision is distinctive. As noted above, the rights-compliant interpretation provision is expressly made subject to the purposive test. I do not see

---

[49] See *Hansen* supra esp at [92] and [192]. See Andrew Butler and Petra Butler, *The New Zealand Bill of Rights Act: A Commentary*, LexisNexis, Wellington, 2005, esp [7.19] and Hanna Wilberg, 'The Bill of Rights and Other Enactments' [2007] *New Zealand Law Journal* 112.

how it could be suggested that, in the light of this factor, the English approach could be applicable, particularly the reasoning that permits a court to override the actual intention of Parliament when passing other legislation.

The same may well be true of the formulation in the current Victorian *Charter*, and the amendment in the ACT, arising from the words 'consistently with their purpose'. These words do not exist in s 3 of the United Kingdom Act. They are words of limitation which, at least, arguably, would not permit the approach that has been adopted in the United Kingdom.

I note that the ACT Court of Appeal has identified both s 139 of the *Legislation Act* (i.e. the purposive requirement), and s 30(1) of the *Human Rights Act* 2004 (i.e. the rights-compliant requirement), as each having a similar form to s 3 of the UK *Human Rights Act* 1998, as explained by the House of Lords in *Ghaidan*. However, the interrelationship between ss 30(1) and 139 of the ACT legislation was not considered.[50]

Chief Justice Higgins of the Supreme Court of the Australian Capital Territory invoked the interpretation provision of the ACT Act when determining the proper interpretation of a section of the *Domestic Violence and Protection Orders Act* 2001 (ACT), which had the effect that

---

50 See *Kingsley's Chicken Pty Ltd v. Queensland Investment Corporation* [2006] ACTCA 9 at [49]–[51].

an interim personal protection order automatically became a final personal protection order, without a hearing and without the prospect of further review. Invoking s 30 of the ACT *Human Rights Act,* his Honour held that the relevant provision empowered, but did not mandate, the making of the final order and did not preclude a respondent to an *ex parte* order from applying to set it aside as of right, if irregularly made, and as a matter of discretion, if cause be shown.[51]

It may be that the principle of legality would have been deployed to similar effect. However, s 30 was more clearly applicable.

The clear statement principle

The determination that the principle of legality, or that a statutorily adopted human right, applies in a particular case is, regrettably, the easy part of the process. All that we have done at this stage is to identity the two elements – namely the statutory formulation and the right – that may give rise to an incompatibility or tension. The difficult part is determining which must prevail in the particular circumstances. It is at this point that judicial reasoning often becomes fuzzy when identifying a relevant test and, perhaps more significantly, when applying it. The relevant test is, more often

---

51 See *SI bhnf CC v. KS bhnf IS* (2005) 195 FLR 151 esp at [71]–[72], [98], [112]–[113].

than not, expressed in the conclusion rather than in the reasoning.

The relevant principle of the law of statutory interpretation, applicable to each principle in the common law bill of rights, is the principle of clear statement. There are a range of verbal formulations, all basically equivalent, that express the presumption that Parliament does not intend to interfere with rights within the principle of legality. I have compiled the following list from the judgments of the High Court of Australia over the years:

> 'Clear and unambiguous words', 'unambiguously clear', 'irresistible clearness', 'express words of plain intendment', 'clear words or necessary implication', 'unmistakable and unambiguous', 'expressly stated or necessarily to be implied', 'clearly emerges whether by express words or by necessary implication', 'with a clearness which admits of no doubt' and 'something unequivocal must be found, either in the context or the circumstances, to overcome the presumption'.[52]

It is often said that a statute which impinges upon the principle of legality, or any of its constituent interpretative principles, must be construed strictly. However, the idea

---

52 See *Durham Holdings Pty Ltd v. New South Wales* (1999) 47 NSWLR 340 at [44]–[45].

of 'strict' construction does not involve a simple standard. There are degrees of strictness. There is very little discussion in the literature or case law about what is meant by strict construction.

I believe we should stop using the language of 'strict construction'. It suggests that courts give a restricted interpretation to the language of Parliament and do so irrespective of the intention of Parliament. That this has been the case, and not only in the distant past, is a good reason for ensuring that the terminology more accurately reflects the true judicial role. In my opinion, this approach is more appropriately called 'the clear statement principle'. All the formulations I have listed reflect this principle.

If Parliament wishes to interfere where rights, liberties and expectations are affected, it must do so with clarity. The clear statement principle is the critical way that the law of statutory interpretation reflects and implements the principle of legality.

A core difficulty remains. Clarity, like beauty, always involves questions of degree and is affected by the eye of the beholder. Significantly the degree of clarity required may vary from right to right and, with respect to any particular right, may vary from time to time.

This was expressly referred to in the joint judgment of the High Court in *Bropho,* in the context of whether a statute binds the Crown, where their Honours said:

> If such an assumption be shown to be or to have become ill-founded, the foundation upon which the particular presumption rests will necessarily be weakened or removed. Thus, if what was previously accepted as a fundamental principle or fundamental right ceases to be so regarded, the presumption of the legislature which would not have intended to depart from that principle or to abolish or modify that right will necessarily be undermined and may well disappear.[53]

It is equally possible that matters that were once regarded as rights, albeit not of a fundamental character, may come to be regarded as more significant than they once were.

When an international human rights instrument is adopted by statute, it may be that a cognate common law right may be given enhanced salience. Indeed, there is a vibrant debate on whether, and if so to what degree, executive ratification of international human rights instruments has such an effect.

The principle of clear statement that has been applied to the common law bill of rights is reflected in American jurisprudence where there is a clear interaction between

---

53 See *Bropho v. Western Australia* (1990) 171 CLR 1 at 18.

constitutional and quasi-constitutional principles.[54] This approach is reflected in the doctrine of 'strict scrutiny' developed for applying the Constitutional Bill of Rights. The United States Supreme Court has adopted what are described as three 'standards of review' which, in ascending order of stringency are: the rational relationship test, the intermediate test and the strict scrutiny test.[55]

When determining the constitutional validity of legislation, the court may employ the standard of least stringency, the rational basis test, whereby the court gives deference to the legislative decision as to whether or not the legislation falls within a head of power. On the intermediate standard of review, there is less deference and the court will require a substantial relationship to an important government interest. The strict scrutiny test, which represents the highest level of judicial review, is the one the court applies whenever the legislative scheme involves what the court classifies as fundamental constitutional rights.

---

[54] See William N Eskridge Jr and Philip P Frickey, 'Quasi-Constitutional Law: Clear Statement Rules as Constitutional Lawmaking' (1992) 45 *Vanderbilt Law Review* 593; Cass R Sunstein, 'Interpreting Statutes in the Regulatory State' (1989) 103 *Harvard Law Review* 405 at 462 (pt IV).

[55] See John E Nowak and Ronald D Rotunda, *Constitutional Law,* 4th edn, West Publishing Co, St Paul, 1991, pp. 574–576; Laurence H Tribe, *American Constitutional Law*, 2nd edn, Foundation Press, New York, 1988: see esp. the index under Rational Relationship Test, Intermediate Scrutiny and Strict Scrutiny.

On this last standard of review the court independently determines the degree of relationship which the law bears to an objective that is constitutionally sanctioned. It is often applied whenever the exercise of a fundamental right is involved, so that the proponent of the legislation must demonstrate that the statute serves a compelling government interest that could not be served by any less restrictive measure. There is much scope for disputation with respect to the application of these tests.[56]

An American constitutional scholar has recently observed:

> [I]n its insistence that any infringement of fundamental rights must be necessary or narrowly tailored to compelling governmental interests, the strict scrutiny formula possesses important commonalities with (though possibly also some important differences from) the similarly generic 'proportionality' tests applied in Germany, Canada, and Israel and by the European Court of Justice. Each of these proportionality tests encompasses three doctrinal subtests, all of which must be satisfied for legislation to survive judicial review. The first asks whether a legislative measure restricting basic rights is

56 See, e.g., Hans A Linde, 'The Shell Game of 'Interest' Scrutiny: Who Must Know What, When, and How?' (1992) 55 *Albany Law Review* 725 at 734; Peter J Reuben, 'Reconnecting Doctrine and Purpose: A Comprehensive Approach to Strict Scrutiny After *Adarand* and *Shaw*' (2000) 149 *University of Pennsylvania Law Review* 1.

> rationally related to a desired end. The second, called 'the principle of necessity' in Germany and 'the least injurious means test' in Israel, requires that the means, 'even if rationally connected to the objective . . . should impair "as little as possible" the right or freedom in question.' The third, called the principle of 'proportionality *stricto sensu'* in Germany and the 'proportionate means test' in Israel, invites the court to balance societal interests against individual rights by asking whether an infringement of rights is proportionate to the desired objective.
>
> I should emphasise, however, that although the strict scrutiny and proportionality tests both aspire to find a middle way between treating rights as absolutes and deferring routinely to legislative compromises of civil liberties, there may be important differences between them. By inviting assessments of all-things-considered reasonableness, proportionality inquiries may tend to deprive rights of any 'special force as trumps,' whereas the American approach, on at least some interpretations, preserves a special, trumping aura for preferred rights.[57]

The status of a Human Rights Charter as a quasi-constitutional text may lead to reliance upon such constitutional analysis in its application. Just as these are 'statutes

---

57 Richard H Fallon Jr, 'Strict Judicial Scrutiny' (2007) 54 *UCLA Law Review* 1267 at 1295–1296.

and statutes', so are there 'rights and rights'. The right to life is not the same kind of right as the right to a speedy trial.

When applying s 3 of the UK Act, it is clear that British judges are not constrained by anything like the principle of clear statement. There is, however, a real issue as to how far beyond that principle the Australian rights-compliant interpretation provisions can be said to go.

Al-Kateb

The Australian case that perhaps most directly raises the issues of statutory interpretation that I have been discussing is *Al-Kateb*, where the High Court split four to three. There appears to have developed a habit of deploying in the title and in sections of legislation, terminology that bears the characteristics of a press release or political statement. In that vein the relevant legislation classified the appellant in *Al-Kateb* as 'an unlawful non-citizen'. The issue was whether he could be detained for the purpose of deportation when there was no present prospect of deportation,[58] because he was stateless and no one would take him.

The relevant statutory provisions were in mandatory language:

- An officer 'must detain' an unlawful non-citizen.
- An unlawful non-citizen 'must be kept in immigration

[58] See *Al-Kateb v. Godwin* (2004) 219 CLR 562 ('*Al-Kateb*').

detention until he or she is . . . removed from Australia'.

- An officer 'must remove, as soon as reasonably practical, an unlawful non-citizen' after a request for removal.

On the facts of the case there was no prospect of Australia receiving international co-operation for the removal of the appellant. By a majority of four to three the High Court held that he could be detained indefinitely. The majority held that there was no room in this context for the application of a 'purposive limitation' or of the presumption that Parliament does not intend to interfere with individual rights and freedoms. Detention must continue until deportation, however unlikely that may be. The terminology, the majority concluded, was clear, unambiguous and intractable.[59]

The minority of Gleeson CJ, Gummow and Kirby JJ, a singular and, as far as I am aware, unique concatenation of dissentients, read down the words 'must be kept in immigration detention'.

Gleeson CJ applied the principle that for a statute to justifiably interfere with human rights or freedoms, it must do so in 'unambiguous language' which indicates 'that the legislature has directed its attention to the rights or freedoms in question and has consciously decided upon

---

59 *Al-Kateb* at [33] per McHugh J; at [241] per Hayne J (with whom Heydon J agreed); and at [298] per Callinan J.

abrogation or curtailment'.[60] The majority made no reference to this particular requirement, which was expressly stated in the joint judgment of the Court in *Coco*.[61] The majority reasoning proceeded on the basis that the mandatory requirement – 'must be kept in immigration detention' – satisfied any such test.

Gummow J construed the provisions as having the purpose of removal and, accordingly, that the power could be read down once that purpose was no longer pertinent.[62]

Kirby J agreed with Gummow J, but also invoked a presumption of the common law 'in favour of liberty and against indefinite detention'.[63]

A recent article speculates about the effect upon the outcome in *Al-Kateb* if a statutory provision equivalent to s 32 of the Victorian *Charter* had been in place. It is reasonably clear that the author does not regard *Al-Kateb* as the high point of contemporary High Court jurisprudence. She is not alone in this. Subject, perhaps, to the current form of the ACT provision, it appears likely that the author is correct when she concludes that a different result would probably have ensued.[64]

---

60 ibid., [19].

61 See *Coco* at [437].

62 ibid., [117] and [122].

63 ibid., [15].

64 See Alice Rolls, 'Avoiding Tragedy: Would the Decision of the High Court in *Al-Kateb* have been any Different if Australia had a Bill of Rights like Victoria?' (2007) 18 *Public Law Review* 119.

The rights-compliant interpretation provisions do go further than the principle of legality. Both the common law bill of rights and the adopted international rights instrument identify personal liberty as a fundamental right, which any system of detention necessarily infringes. The express statutory requirement to interpret the words of other legislation so as to comply with an express statutory right is, in my opinion, more likely to be given effect than a judge-made principle derived only from Parliament's presumed intention. The words of the statute will be assessed by Parliament's express intention.

One does not have to go as far as the English judiciary has gone to give force and effect to an expression of Parliamentary will in a statute entitled to be treated as quasi-constitutional. The inhibition that any judge will feel, albeit to varying degrees, before trespassing into what may appear to some to be the province of the Parliament, must be allayed to some degree by such an express Parliamentary mandate.

This is particularly so because of the requirement, in the Australian form of the interpretation provision, to have regard to the purpose of the legislation. In *Al-Kateb* it was quite clear that detention for the purpose of deportation could not be attained because, on the facts, deportation could not occur in the foreseeable future. I think it likely that some members of the majority may have found the language less intractable if they had had an express statutory requirement to interpret the statutory language so as to validate the appellant's right to personal liberty.

As the dissentients in *Al-Kateb* show, such a result is well within the permissible scope of interpretation. Whether the English position can be so described will be discussed in the third lecture.

LEGITIMATE AND SPURIOUS INTERPRETATION

CHAPTER THREE

LEGITIMATE AND SPURIOUS INTERPRETATION

On 31 March 1717 Benjamin Hoadly, the Bishop of Bangor, delivered a sermon before George I of Great Britain entitled 'The Nature of the Kingdom of Christ'. His text was John 18:36, 'My Kingdom is not of this world'. His sermon ignited what became known as the Bangorian Controversy, named after Hoadly's see. The appellation was conferred apparently without irony, although the central message of his sermon was that there was no biblical justification for *any* form of Church government, which presumably excluded bishoprics. He proclaimed that Christ had not delegated his authority to any representative, no doubt including all bishops. His theological position proved attractive to George I and George II, who acted as his patrons and protected him from his episcopal colleagues.

In the course of denying the right of any person to intercede between the ultimate source of sovereignty and the individual worshipper, Bishop Hoadly proclaimed a theory denying any right of interpretation. He said:

> Whoever hath an absolute authority to interpret any written or spoken laws, it is he who is truly the lawgiver, to all intents and purposes, and not the person who first spoke or wrote them.[1]

American realist interpretation scholars who are fond of quoting Hoadly[2] do not make it clear that the bishop was concerned only with a text which reveals the word of God and which, accordingly, cannot be amended. He expressly excluded secular legislation, which can be changed if interpreted wrongly. Nevertheless, as in the case of a written constitution, that ability may sometimes be more theoretical than real.

The dictum of Bishop Hoadly reflects views sometimes expressed by those who emphasise the purity of other sovereign authority, whether parliamentary sovereignty or the sovereign people. We can refer to this as the Bangorian

---

1 Reprinted in John M Creed and SB Smith, *Religious Thought in the Eighteenth Century*, Cambridge University Press, Cambridge, 1934, p. 251.

2 Quoted by John Gray, *The Nature and Sources of Law*, 2nd edn, Macmillan, New York, 1921, p. 125.

school of statutory interpretation. It is reflected in the Benthamite approach, common in civil law jurisdictions, that understanding legislation is a simple mechanical task. That has never been the common law tradition.

Notwithstanding the fulminations of parliamentary drafters, who often proclaim the obviousness of their intent and the clarity of their words which a court has misunderstood, the process of statutory interpretation has always been regarded as raising real issues that require analysis. Unlike the civil law we have never had a 'Low Court' tradition, equivalent to the 'Low Church' tradition represented by Bishop Hoadly.

The contrast in approach appears, perhaps most notably, by comparing typical judgments of common law courts with those of civil law courts. In the former, reasons are set forth in full. In most civil law jurisdictions, though there have been changes in this respect in some over recent decades, the reasons for judgment are curt, by reason of the pretence that all that has to be done is a mechanical application of the words of a code. This comparative lack of transparency in the true process of reasoning that led to a result, explains to a significant degree why the bureaucratised judiciary in many civil law countries does not have the status, nor the respect of the public, to the degree to which we have become accustomed.

Even the three basic rules of traditional formulation: the

literal rule, the golden rule and the mischief rule – which, as I have said in my first lecture have contemporary echoes in textualism, contextualism and purposive interpretation respectively – were each regarded as legitimate. They did not, indeed could not, lead to the same result. The choice of which rule to apply often involved a dialectic process in an intellectual tradition which can be traced back over five centuries.

The Austinian approach

As I indicated in the first lecture, the salience that human rights considerations have acquired over recent decades represents the resurgence of natural law and the partial demise of legal positivism. In the nineteenth century when legal positivism replaced the remnant of natural law thinking in the English common law tradition, one of the battlegrounds was statutory interpretation.

In his *Lectures on Jurisprudence,* the foundational text of legal positivism, John Austin denounced what he called 'spurious interpretation'.[3] To make his position quite clear he further characterised this approach as 'bastard interpretation'. He said:

---

3 See John Austin, *Lectures on Jurisprudence*, 4th edn, John Murray, London, 1879, vol 2, pp. 1029–1030.

> There is a species of interpretation or construction (or rather of judicial legislation disguised with the name of interpretation) by which the defective but clear provisions of a statute are extended to a case which those provisions have omitted . . . [*T*]*his* species of interpretation or construction is *not* interpretation or construction properly so called . . . [A]dopting the current but absurd expression, the judge *interprets* the law *extensively*, in pursuance of its reason or principle.
>
> The so-called interpretation . . . is widely different from the *genuine* extensive interpretation which takes the reason of the law as its index or guide. In the latter case, the reason or general design is unaffectedly employed as a *mean* for discovering or ascertaining the specific and doubtful intention. In the former case the reason or principle of the statute is itself erected into a law, and is applied to a *species* or case which the lawgiver has manifestly overlooked.[4]

The approach to statutory interpretation to which Austin was responding had come to be referred to as the 'equity of the statute'. This was a doctrine pursuant to which the courts sought to effectuate the will of Parliament by extending the operation of a statute in accordance with the

---

4 ibid., 596–597.

justice of a particular case.[5] Insofar as the doctrine operated to restrict the scope of a statute, the approach is still applied today. However, insofar as the doctrine was used to extend the scope of the statute, that is a matter of some controversy which I will discuss below.

The doctrine of the equity of a statute reflects the historical origins of the institutions of government in the British system. Originally the King met in Council and there was no distinction between legislative, executive and judicial functions. Over time the Council, originally comprised of the nobility only, developed into the Parliament as we know it. A committee of councillors, wielding the executive power, developed into the Cabinet as we know it. The judicial power came to be exercised by specialist judges, rather than by the King in Council and the prerogative courts like Star Chamber and High Commission disappeared or, like Chancery, were judicialised. The very word 'court' reflects the origin of the judicial function amongst those in the immediate presence of a King.

Over the centuries, when statutes were in fact quite uncommon, Parliament was regarded primarily as a court in

---

[5] For a general discussion of this doctrine, together with references, see WMC Gummow, *Change and Continuity: Statute, Equity, and Federalism*, Oxford University Press, Oxford, 1999, pp. 18–22; see also his Honour's joint judgment with Justice Deane in *Nelson v. Nelson* (1995) 184 CLR 538 at 552–554.

the modern sense. That has clearly changed. More significantly, for most of those centuries, judges were regarded as a manifestation of executive authority. Indeed judges often drafted the statutes.[6] As a thirteenth-century Chief Justice, Ralf de Hengham, once berated a pleader: 'Do not gloss the statute; we understand it better than you, for we made it.'[7]

The doctrine of equity of the statute reflected this admixture of functions and, as has recently been comprehensively established,[8] it is quite inconsistent with a separation of powers of the contemporary character, whether as strict as Article III of the US Constitution or Chapter 3 of the Australian Constitution, or of the more flexible kind which applies, for example, in the United Kingdom and in the Australian states.

Although reference is made to the equity of the statute approach in Blackstone's *Commentaries*, by his time the emphasis was plainly on judicial interpretation in the contemporary sense. Judges sought to identify the intention of the legislature.

---

6 See P St J Langan, *Maxwell on the Interpretation of Statutes*, 12th edn, Sweet & Maxwell, London, 1969, p. 237; Francis Bennion, *Statutory Interpretation: A Code*, 4th edn, Butterworths, London, 2002, Section 159.

7 T F T Plucknett, *Statutes and their Interpretation in the First Half of the Fourteenth Century*, Cambridge University Press, Cambridge, 1992, p. 95.

8 See John F Manning, 'Textualism and the Equity of the Statute' (2001) 101 *Columbia Law Review* 1. For an earlier but shorter statement of this position see Roscoe Pound, 'Spurious Interpretation' (1907) 1 *Columbia Law Review* 379 esp at 383–384.

One American author on statutory interpretation has classified judicial approaches to interpretation in the following manner:

- textualists who give precedence to the literal words of the text;
- purposivists who employ purpose to clarify an ambiguous text;
- strong purposivists who rely on purpose to depart from a clear statutory text.[9]

All three categories, nevertheless, find their rationale in what the author describes as the 'faithful agent theory'. He went on to distinguish the revival of interest in the 'equity of the statute' of a traditional character, which had some residual support at the time of the creation of the United States, not least in Blackstone's *Commentaries* which were so influential at the time. If there was an inherent judicial power to adapt legislation at the time of the formulation of the Constitution of the United States, this would be a form of interpretation attractive to originalists, who have in the past tended to be strong textualists. The author sets out a convincing refutation of this theory.

The traditional equity of the statute approach has had a residual influence on the law of statutory interpretation. Justice Gummow has identified a number of principles

---

9 See Manning supra esp. at 3ff.

of interpretation as continuing the equity of the statute approach under different terminology.[10] Justice Finn of the Federal Court has expressed a similar opinion[11] and, his Honour notes, the statutory requirement to prefer an interpretation which promotes the purpose or object underlying an act may be seen as reflecting at least in part a similar process.

The resurgence of interest in human rights does raise again the Austinian distinction between genuine and spurious interpretation. This is reflected in debates about judicial activism, in debates about whether to adopt a bill of rights and in debates about the judicial implementation of a bill of rights. The determination of when interpretation has become 'spurious' is a matter upon which reasonable minds can and will differ. It is, however, a real issue.

About a century ago Roscoe Pound developed and commented upon the Austinian concept of spurious interpretation. Its contemporary relevance makes it worthy of extensive quotation:

> The difficulty calling for interpretation may be
> (a) which of two or more coordinate rules to apply, or

---

10 Gummow supra.

11 Paul Finn, 'Statutes and the Common Law: The Continuing Story' in Suzanne Corcoran and Stephen Bottomley (eds), *Interpreting Statutes*, Federation Press, Sydney, 2005, p. 52 at 57–58.

(b) to determine what the lawmaker intended to prescribe by a given rule, or (c) to meet deficiencies or excesses in rules imperfectly conceived or enacted. The first two are cases for genuine interpretation. The third case, when treated as a matter of interpretation, calls for spurious interpretation.

The object of genuine interpretation is to discover the rule which the lawmaker intended to establish; to discover the intention with which the lawmaker made the rule, or the sense which he attached to the words wherein the rule is expressed . . . Employed for these purposes, interpretation is purely judicial in character; and so long as the ordinary means of interpretation, namely the literal meaning of the language used in the context, are resorted to, there can be no question. But when, as often happens, these primary indices to the meaning and intention of the lawmaker fail to lead to a satisfactory result, and recourse must be had to the reason and spirit of the rule, or to the intrinsic merit of the several possible interpretations, the line between a genuine ascertaining of the meaning of the law, and the making over of the law under the guise of interpretation, becomes more difficult. Strictly, both are means of genuine interpretation. They are not covers for the making of new law. They are modes of arriving at the real intent of the maker of existing law. The former

> means of interpretation tries to find out directly what the lawmaker meant by assuming his position, in the surroundings in which he acted, and endeavouring to gain from the mischiefs he had to meet and the remedy by which he sought to meet them, his intention with respect to the particular point in controversy. The latter, if the former fails to yield sufficient light, seeks to reach the intent of the lawmaker indirectly . . .
>
> On the other hand, the object of spurious interpretation is to make, unmake, or remake, and not merely to discover. It puts a meaning into the text as a juggler puts coins, or what not, into a dummy's hair, to be pulled forth presently with an air of discovery. It is essentially a legislative, not a judicial process . . . [12]

Pound characterised spurious interpretation as an anachronism in an age of statutes and also as inconsistent with the separation of powers.

The current version of the equity of the statute approach manifests itself as 'dynamic interpretation'. A principal United States proponent of this approach described it thus:

---

12 Pound supra at 381–382.

Because they are aimed at big problems and must last a long time, statutory enactments are often general, abstract and theoretical. Interpretation of a statute usually occurs in connection with a fact-specific problem (a case or an administrative record) which renders it relatively particular, concrete and practical. As an exercise in practical rather than theoretical reasoning, statutory interpretation will be dynamic. It is a truism that interpretation depends heavily on context, but the elasticity of context is less well recognised. The expanded context of cases and problems engenders dynamic interpretation. Because statutes have an indefinite life, they apply to fact situations well into the future. When successive applications of the statute occur in context not anticipated by its authors, the statute's meaning evolves *beyond* original expectations. Indeed, sometimes in subsequent applications reveal that factual or legal assumptions of the original statute have become (or were originally) erroneous; then the statute's meaning often evolves *against* its original expectations.[13]

[13] William N Eskridge Jr, *Dynamic Statutory Interpretation*, Harvard University Press, Cambridge Mass, 1994, pp. 48–49.

This 'dynamic' approach has been noted with approval in Australia.[14] Lady Justice Arden has applied a similar, but not identical, distinction by way of characterisation of the effect given to s 3 of the *Human Rights Act* of the United Kingdom by the English cases I discussed in the second lecture.[15] Her Ladyship said:

> [25] What does the interpretative duty mean in practice? Significantly, in relation to the interpretation of legislation under the *Human Rights Act* 1998, we move from an Agency Model to the 'Dynamic Model'. The judge is not simply looking at the wording and trying to apply it. He is looking at the wording critically. He is considering whether it complies with the Convention. This approach works on the basis that what Parliament intended was that statutes should have the effect of operating in conformity with human rights unless the contrary conclusion could not be achieved as a matter of interpretation. But, in truth, it is no longer a matter of looking at Parliamentary intention. This is highlighted by the fact that new

---

14 See Suzanne Corcoran, 'Theories of Statutory Interpretation' in Corcoran and Bottomley supra 8 at 21–25 and Suzanne Corcoran 'The Architecture of Interpretation: Dynamic Practice and Constitutional Principles' passim in Corcoran and Bottomley supra 31.

15 Mary Arden, 'The Changing Judicial Role: Human Rights, Community Law and the Intention of Parliament', Annual Lecture to the Constitutional and Administrative Law Bar Association, London, 26 November 2007.

> approach applies to legislation whenever passed. At the highest level of generality, the court is acting as the guardian of human rights and constitutional rights. Its role is a dynamic one, and hence I call the model in this context the Dynamic Model.

Her Ladyship goes on to discuss the implications of what she calls the Dynamic Model for the role of the judiciary.

This development in England raises many of the issues to which Roscoe Pound referred a century ago. It appears that in jurisdictions from which Australians once drew guidance, including both the United Kingdom and Canada, the dominant view may differ from ours. In Australia the debate is still continuing.

The limits of interpretation

The application of the principles listed in the Common Law Bill of Rights, the subject of the first lecture, and the application of the rights-compliant interpretation provisions, the subject of the second lecture, raise analogous, indeed probably identical, issues about the judicial role. Determining the boundary between interpretation and legislation arises in both respects.

The English case law on their rights-compliant interpretation provision, discussed in the second lecture, goes beyond what most Australian judges would regard as 'interpretation'. English judges are, of course, well aware that there is a constitutional boundary beyond which they should not travel. They recognise that interpretation cannot become, in substance, amendment of legislation.

Lord Nicholls identified the issue in the following manner:

> [38] . . . Section 3 is concerned with interpretation . . . and, indeed, section 3(2)(b) presuppose[s] that not all provisions in primary legislation can be read Convention compliant by the application of section 3(1) . . .
>
> [39] In applying section 3 courts must be ever mindful of this outer limit. The *Human Rights Act* reserves the amendment of primary legislation to Parliament. By this means the Act seeks to preserve parliamentary sovereignty. The Act maintains the constitutional boundary. Interpretation of statutes is a matter for the courts; the enactment of statutes, and the amendment of statutes, are matters for Parliament.
>
> [40] Up to this point there is no difficulty. The area of real difficulty lies in identifying the limits of interpretation in a particular case. This is not a novel problem . . . What one person regards as sensible, if robust, interpretation, another regards as impermissibly

> creative. For present purposes it is sufficient to say that a meaning which departs substantially from a fundamental feature of an Act of Parliament is likely to have crossed the boundary between interpretation and amendment.[16]

Lord Bingham's judgment in *Sheldrake*, quoted in my second lecture, synthesised the English authorities. His Lordship indicated clearly that there were limits to the deployment of s 3 and outlined a number of formulations identifying those limits, including:

- 'Inconsistent with a fundamental feature of legislation';[17]
- 'Incompatible with the underlying thrust of the legislation';[18]
- 'Change the substance of a provision completely';[19] and
- 'Remove the very core and essence, "pith and substance" of the measure Parliament had enacted'.[20]

To an Australian judge, those are not restrictive criteria. Because of the express reference to the purpose of

---

16 *Re S (children: care plan); Re W (children: care plan)* [2002] 2 AC 291.

17 *Ghaidan v. Godin-Mendoza* [2004] 2 AC 557 ('*Ghaidan*') at [32] per Lord Steyn and at [67]–[68] per Lord Millett.

18 ibid., [33] per Lord Steyn.

19 ibid., [110] per Lord Rodger.

20 ibid., [111].

Parliament – either by express subjection in the current ACT formulation or in terms of 'consistency' in the Victorian and new ACT formulation – Australian provisions differ in a critical respect from that of the UK. What is regarded as 'interpretation' in England would not necessarily be so regarded here, even under the rights-compliant interpretation provisions. English case law must be deployed with care.

In the first lecture I identified a range of processes which come within an orthodox statement of the interpretative task:

- deciding the meaning of ambiguous or obscure words;
- deciding whether to read down general words;
- deciding whether implications are to be drawn from a text;
- considering whether to depart from the natural and ordinary meaning of words by adoption of a strained construction;
- deciding whether or not a statutory deposition does not apply on the basis of an intention to the contrary;
- giving qualificatory words an ambulatory operation; and
- reading words into a statute by filling gaps (more controversially).

In the time available I propose to discuss three of these processes as they often arise in the application of the principle of legality and of rights-compliant interpretation provisions. These are: strained construction, reading down general words and reading words into a statute.

Strained construction

There are numerous references in the authorities to the permissibility of adopting, in particular circumstances, what is described as a 'strained construction' of statutory language. Bennion, in accordance with the requirements of the approach of his text as a 'code', identifies strained construction with any approach which fails to implement a clear grammatical meaning or one of the possible grammatical meanings.[21] An appropriate statement of strained interpretation in a purposive context is that of Lord Justice MacKinnon who said:

> When the purpose of an enactment is clear, it is often legitimate, because it is necessary, to put a strained interpretation upon some words which have been inadvertently used, and of which the plain meaning would defeat the obvious intention of the legislature. It may even be necessary, and therefore legitimate, to

---

[21] See Bennion supra at Sections 157 to 159. See also Sections 190 and 306.

substitute for an inept word or words that which such intention requires.[22]

In Australia the most systematic statement of circumstances in which a strained interpretation is appropriate is that of Justice McHugh, first in the Court of Appeal of New South Wales and then in the High Court.[23] I will deal separately with the processes of reading down general words and reading words into a statute. His Honour identified circumstances in which a strained construction has been adopted as including:

- where the operation of the statute appears to be absurd, capricious or irrational;[24]
- where terminology has been inadvertently used;[25]
- where words have been omitted, particularly words which constitute a failure to deal with an eventuality required to be dealt with if the purpose of the act is to

---

22 *Sutherland Publishing Co Ltd v. Caxton Publishing Co Ltd* [1938] Ch 174 ('*Sutherland Publishing*') at 201.

23 See *Kingston v. Keprose Pty Ltd (No 3)* (1987) 11 NSWLR 404 ('*Kingston v. Keprose*') esp at 421–423; *Mills v. Meeking* (1990) 169 CLR 214 ('*Mills v. Meeking*') at 242–243; *Saraswati v. The Queen* (1991) 172 CLR 1 ('*Saraswati*') at 21–23.

24 See e.g., *Cooper-Brookes (Wollongong) Pty Ltd v. Federal Commissioner of Taxation* (1981) 147 CLR 297 ('*Cooper-Brookes*') at 321 quoted and applied by McHugh J in *Saraswati* at 22; *Re Lockwood* [1958] Ch 231 at 238 quoted in *Kingston v. Keprose* at 422.

25 See *Sutherland Publishing* at 201 quoted in *Kingston v. Keprose* at 422.

be achieved;[26] and

- where the purpose of the provision indicates that Parliament did not intend the grammatical meaning to apply.[27]

Nevertheless, in each respect, what must be undertaken is a process of interpretation and this imposes a significant restraint upon the ability of a court to effectuate what the court identifies to be the true legislative purpose.

The task of the court is to interpret the words used by Parliament. It is not to divine the intent of the Parliament.[28] The courts must determine what Parliament meant by the words it used. The courts do not determine what Parliament intended to say.[29]

---

[26] See *Kammins Ballrooms Co Ltd v. Zenith Investments (Torquay) Ltd* [1971] AC 850 at 880-882; *Jones v. Wrotham Park Settled Estates* [1980] AC 74 ('*Jones v. Wrotham Park*') at 105.

[27] *Adler v. George* [1964] 2 QB 7; *Wiltshire v. Barrett* [1966] 1 QB 312 at 332–333 referred to in *Kingston v Keprose* at 422.

[28] See *State v. Zuma* (1995) (4) BCLR 401 at 402; [1995] (2) SA 642; *Matadeen v. Pointu* [1999] 1 AC 98 at 108; *R v. PLV* (2001) 51 NSWLR 736 at [82]; *La Compagnie Sucriere de Bel Ombre Ltee v. Government of Mauritius* (Unreported, Privy Council, 13 December 1995); *Pinder v. The Queen* [2003] 1 AC 620 at [24].

[29] *R v. Bolton; Ex parte Beane* (1987) 162 CLR 514 at 518; *Byrne v. Australian Airlines Ltd* (1995) 185 CLR 410 at 459; *Wik Peoples v. Queensland* (1996) 187 CLR 1 at 168–169; *Stock v. Frank Jones (Tipton) Ltd* [1978] 1 All ER 948 at 953d; [1978] 1 WLR 231 at 236G; *Black-Clawson International Ltd v. Papierwerke Waldhof-Aschaffenburg AC* [1975] AC 591 at 613G, 645C–V; *R v. Young* (1999) 46 NSWLR 681 at [5]; *Dossett v. TKJ Nominees Pty Ltd* (2003) 218 CLR 1 at [10]; *Donselear v. Donselear* (1982) 1 NZLR 97 at 114.

A good example of permissible strained construction is a recent judgment of the Queensland Court of Appeal as to whether an unregistered motor cycle was subject to the indemnity provisions of the *Motor Accidents Insurance Act* 1994 (Qld). The definition of a motor vehicle supported the insurer's contention that the obligation to indemnify applied only to registered uninsured vehicles, but not to unregistered uninsured vehicles. Nothing could be more clearly inconsistent with the purpose of compulsory third party insurance. The difficulty arose because the obligation to indemnify for an uninsured motor vehicle was expressed in terms of an accident 'on a road or in a public place', whereas the obligation to register a vehicle was expressed in terms only of use 'on a road', without reference to a 'public place'. By means of a strained interpretation, the reference to motor vehicle was interpreted to include reference to a vehicle for which registration was not required until such time as the regulation required such registration.[30]

This case probably falls into the absurdity or irrationality category. The analysis is a clear application of the relevant principles within proper bounds of the interpretative task.

The limits of strained construction are well expressed by Lord Reid who said:

---

30 See *Nominal Defendant v. Ravenscroft* [2007] QCA 435 ('*Ravenscroft*') esp. at [54]–[55].

> It is a cardinal principle applicable to all kinds of statutes that you may not for any reason attach to a statutory provision a meaning which the words of that provision cannot reasonably bear. If they are capable of more than one meaning, then you can chose between those meanings, but beyond that you must not go.[31]

I am aware that in the NSW Court of Appeal, Justice McHugh suggested that this passage did not 'express the modern law of statutory interpretation'. However, he did not repeat this statement in the High Court judgments in which he repeated his analysis.[32]

McHugh JA's characterisation of Lord Reid's reasoning has not been subsequently adopted. Indeed, the joint judgment of Mason and Wilson JJ in *Cooper-Brookes,* which is usually cited, including by McHugh J, as the basis of contemporary Australian doctrine in this regard, expressly adopted a 'reasonably open' test when their Honours said:

---

31 *Jones v. Director of Public Prosecutions* [1962] AC 635 at 662.

32 Cf *Kingston v. Keprose* at 422–423; *Mills v. Meeking*; *Saraswati*; *Newcastle City Council v. GIO General Ltd* (1997) 191 CLR 85 ('*Newcastle v. GIO*'). I note further that McHugh JA's criticism of what he said were observations to the same effect by Viscount Symonds in *Magor and St Mellons Rural District Council v. Newport Corporation* [1952] AC 189 and have not generally found favour. See, e.g., *Footscray City College v. Ruzicka* (2007) 16 VR 498 ('*Ruzicka*') at [67]; *VOAW v. Minister for Immigration and Multicultural and Indigenous Affairs* (2003) 79 ALD 422 ('*VOAW*') at [12]; cf *Ravenscroft* at [34]–[36].

> [T]here are cases in which inconvenience of result or improbability of result assists the court in concluding that an alternative construction *which is reasonably open* is to be preferred to the literal meaning because the alternative interpretation more closely conforms to the legislative intent *discernible from other provisions in the statute.*[33]

A strained construction is sometimes permissible, but the process must be able to be characterised as genuine not spurious interpretation. The overriding test is that the meaning must be reasonably open.

Reading down general words

When should general words used in a statute be read down so as to have a narrower meaning than that of which they are literally capable? It is actually quite rare to find an English word that cannot be applied at different levels of generality or cannot otherwise be circumscribed in its application.

For those who seek comfort in the 'plain meaning' approach, it is necessary to recognise, in the words of Lord Wilberforce, that general words do not necessarily have a 'plain meaning'.[34]

Reading down general words, particularly by the

---

33 *Cooper-Brookes* at 320 (emphasis added).

34 *Maunsell v. Olins* [1975] AC 373 at 385–386.

application of presumptions attributed to the legislature, is a well-established means of statutory interpretation.[35]

As long ago as 1560, in *Stradling v. Morgan* the Barons of the Court of the Exchequer said:

> And the Judges of the law in all times past have so far pursued the intent of the makers of statutes, that they have expounded Acts which were general in words to be but particular where the intent was particular.[36]

A fuller quotation from this judgment of 1560 has a decidedly contemporary ring:

> the sages of the law heretofore have construed statutes quite contrary to the letter in some appearance, and those statutes which comprehend all things in the letter, they have expounded to extend but to some things, and those which generally prohibit all people from doing such an act, they have interpreted to permit some people to do it, and those which include every person in the letter they have adjudged to reach to some persons only, which

---

35 I have collected the relevant Australian authorities in *R v. Young* (1999) 46 NSWLR 681 ('*R v. Young*') at [25]–[31]; JJ Spigelman, 'Statutory Interpretation: Identifying the Linguistic Register' (1999) 4 *Newcastle Law Review* 1 at 8; JJ Spigelman, 'The Poet's Rich Resource: Issues in Statutory Interpretation' (2001) 21 *Australian Bar Review* 224 at 227–230, 232–233.

36 *Stradling v. Morgan* (1560) 1 Plowd 199 at 204; 75 ER 305 at 312.

> expositions have always been founded upon the intent of the Legislature, which they have collected sometimes by considering the cause and necessity of making the Act, sometimes by comparing one part of the Act with another, and sometimes by foreign circumstances. So that they have ever been guided by the intent of the Legislature, which they have always taken according to the necessity of the matter, and according to that which is consonant to reason and good discretion.[37]

Of course, during this period the judges were still under the influence of the doctrine of the equity of the statute. Nevertheless, this technique of interpretation survived the demise of that doctrine. Even in 1890, Lord Halsbury LC described *Stradling v. Morgan* as a 'great case'.[38]

There are numerous examples of reading down that could be cited. Perhaps the best-known example in legal history, from the time when the law of real property was of

---

37 ibid. at Plowd 205; ER 315. See also *Bowtell v. Goldsborough, Mort & Co Ltd* (1905) 3 CLR 444 ('*Bowtell*') at 457–458; *Ex parte Walsh; In re Yates* (1925) 37 CLR 36 ('*Ex parte Walsh*') at 91–93; *R v. Wilson: Ex parte Kisch* (1934) 52 CLR 234 ('*Kisch*') at 244; *Commercial Union Insurance Co Ltd v. Colonial Carrying Co of New Zealand Ltd* [1937] NZLR 1041 at 1047-1049; *Church of the Holy Trinity v. United States,* 143 US 457 (1892) ('*Holy Trinity Church*') at 459; *Tokyo Mart Pty Ltd v. Campbell* (1988) 15 NSWLR 275 at 283; *Smith v. East Elloe Rural District Council* [1956] AC 736 ('*Smith v. East Elloe*') at 764–765; *Bropho v. Western Australia* (1990) 171 CLR 1 at 17-18 ('*Bropho*').

38 *Cox v. Hakes* (1890) 15 App Cas 506 at 517; see also *Hawkins v. Gathercole* (1885) 6 GM&G 1 at 21; 43 ER 1129 at 1135–1136.

central significance to economic and social life, occurred in the context of the Statute of Frauds. The object of requiring contracts for the disposal of land to be in writing was two-fold: first, to avoid fraud and secondly, to ensure certainty. At the expense of the second objective the courts came to give the first object primary significance in what would today be described as a purposive interpretation.

The courts proceeded on the basis that a statute, which had as one purpose the avoidance of fraud, could not be used as 'an engine of fraud' or as an 'instrument of fraud'.[39] After the doctrine of the equity of the statute had receded from judicial memory, one can detect some embarrassment with formulations of this character.[40] An alternative formulation was suggested so that doctrines such as that of part performance, which avoided the strict application of the statute, were necessary because otherwise, in Lord Selbourne's words:

> injustice of a kind which the statute cannot be thought to have had in contemplation would follow on.[41]

As Justice Hope explained the development:

---

[39] See *McCormick v. Grogan* (1869) LR 4 HL 82 at 97.

[40] See, e.g., *Maddison v. Alderson* (1883) 8 App Cas 467 at 474.

[41] ibid., 475.

> No sooner had the *Statute of Frauds* been enacted in 1677 than the courts set about relieving persons of its effect in cases where it was thought that the legislation could not have been intended to apply. In general terms, it was said that the courts would not allow the *Statute of Frauds* to be made an instrument of fraud, and that it did not prevent the proof of fraud . . . The general approach . . . spread into a number of fields where a statute requires writing . . . The fields . . . include, as well as the doctrine of part performance, the rule that parol evidence is admissible to show that an absolute conveyance was in truth by way of security only, the principle that oral evidence can establish that a person has taken a transfer of property as trustee or agent for another, the doctrine whereby equity gave relief upon a breach by the survivor of two persons of a contract they had made to make mutual wills, and the principle whereby equity will compel beneficiaries who have agreed to accept their interests under the will upon communicated trusts to perform those trusts.[42]

In several ways the seemingly absolute requirement of writing was read down on the basis of an imputed intention

---

[42] See *Last v. Rosenfeld* [1972] 2 NSWLR 923 at 927–928.

of Parliament. The process of reading down general words has a rich legal history. It is an acceptable, indeed essential, technique of interpretation.

The operation of the principles of statutory interpretation which I have collectively discussed under the heading 'Common Law Bill of Rights' in the first lecture have often been applied in this way. [43] So will the rights-compliant interpretation provisions discussed in the second lecture.

In the United States the classic application of this approach is an 1892 decision of the United States Supreme Court. The Church of the Holy Trinity in New York contracted with an Englishman to come to the Church as its rector and pastor. The issue was whether this violated a Federal statute which made it unlawful for a person to 'assist or encourage the importation or migration of any alien . . . under contract or agreement . . . to perform labour or service of any kind in the United States'. In finding that the contract was not within the statute the Court said:

> It is a familiar rule, that a thing may be within the letter of the statute and yet not within the statute, because

---

[43] See, e.g., *Bowtell* at 456–457; *Ex parte Walsh* at 91–93; *Kisch* at 244; *Smith v. East Elloe* at 764–765; *Bropho* at 17–18; *R v. Young* at [23]–[32]; *Al-Kateb v. Godwin* (2004) 219 CLR 562 esp at [19], [117], [122].

> not within its spirit, nor within the intention of its makers. This has often been asserted, and the reports are full of cases illustrating its application. This is not the substitution of the will of the judge for that of the legislator, for frequently words of general meaning are used in the statute, words broad enough to include an act in question, and yet a consideration of the whole legislation or of the circumstances surrounding its enactment, or of the absurd results which follow from giving such a broad meaning to the words, makes it unreasonable to believe that the legislator intended to include the particular act.[44]

The Court identified the circumstances which led to the passage of the legislation as a concern with the importation of cheap unskilled labour. Hardly applicable to a man of the cloth.

The Court concluded:

> It is a case where there was presented a definite evil, in view of which the legislature used general terms with the purpose of reaching all phases of that evil, and thereafter, unexpectedly, it is developed that the general language thus employed is broad enough to reach cases and acts

---

44 *Holy Trinity Church* at 459.

> which the whole history and life of a country affirm could not have been intentionally legislated against. It is the duty of the courts, under those circumstances, to say that, however broad the language of the statute may be, the Act, although within the letter, is not within the intention of the legislature, and therefore cannot be within the statute.[45]

Justice Scalia of the United States Supreme Court has attacked the line of authority which includes the *Church of the Holy Trinity* case on the following basis:

> Congress can enact foolish statutes as well as wise ones, and it is not for the courts to decide which is which and rewrite the former . . . *Church of the Holy Trinity* is cited to us whenever counsel wants us to ignore the narrow, deadening text of the statute, and pay attention to the life giving legislative intent. It is nothing but an invitation to judicial law making.[46]

Justice Scalia's approach has not prevailed in the United States, although the new configuration of the majority in the Supreme Court may well indicate increased support

---

45 Ibid at 472.

46 Antonin Scalia, *A Matter of Interpretation: Federal Courts and the Law*, Princeton University Press, Princeton, 1997, pp. 20–21.

for his critique, particularly in the area of constitutional interpretation.

Nevertheless, there are limits to what the Court can do whilst still performing the legitimate task of interpretation. Oliver Wendell Holmes Jr stated the position with his customary epigrammatic brevity. Speaking of a statute which he described as 'a foolish law' – it happened to be the *Sherman Act* – he said: 'If my fellow citizens want to go to Hell, I will help them. It's my job'.[47]

The technique of reading down general provisions can, of course, be used to deny human rights as well as to implement them. In the early twentieth century, the House of Lords and the Privy Council used the technique to frustrate the ambitions of the women's movement in the following ways:[48]

- by reading down the word 'person' in the Act entitling university graduates to vote for the university's seat in Parliament as not including women;[49]
- by holding that the *Sex Disqualification Removal Act* 1917 which provided that no person should be disqualified

---

47 Oliver Wendell Holmes (ed), *Holmes-Laski Letters: The Correspondence of Mr Justice Holmes and Harold J Laski 1916–1935,* Harvard University Press, Cambridge Mass, 1953, p. 219.

48 See generally Andrew Turek, 'Ladies for Life or Who Sits Where?' (1990) 49 *Cambridge Law Journal* 334; Brenda Hale, 'The House of Lords and Women's Rights or Am I Really a Law Lord?' (2005) 25 *Legal Studies* 72.

49 *Nairn v. University of St Andrews* [1909] AC 147.

on the grounds of sex from 'the exercise of any public function' did not extend to modify letters patent of a peerage that permitted male heirs, but not female heirs, to sit in Parliament;[50]

- by overruling the Canadian Supreme Court to hold that the word 'persons' in the section of the *British North America Act* 1876 governing the appointment of new Senators denoted only 'male persons'.[51]

From a human rights perspective, this well-established technique of interpretation can be seen to be neutral, a quality which enhances its contemporary deployment.

Reading words into an act

Some authorities and texts refer to a process of 'reading words into an act'. This terminology appears to me to offend a fundamental principle of our constitutional arrangements. In my opinion, the relevant authorities are consistent with a process of interpretation by which the court interprets the words actually used by the Parliament by giving them effect *as if* they contained additional words which must be complied with or as if some words were deleted for a specific application. This does not, in my opinion, introduce words into the act. It involves the interpretation of the

---

50 *Viscountess Rhondda's Claim* [1922] 2 AC 339.

51 *Edwards v. Attorney General (Can)* [1930] AC 124.

words actually used, perhaps by means of one of the specific techniques of interpretation I have set out above.[52]

The most frequently cited passage to this effect is from Lord Diplock in *Jones v Wrotham Settled Park Estates,* where he sets out restrictive conditions before anything of this character can occur. His Lordship said:

> My Lords, I am not reluctant to adopt a purposive construction where to apply the literal meaning of the legislative language used would lead to results which would clearly defeat the purposes of the Act. But in doing so the task on which a court of justice is engaged remains one of construction, even where this involves reading into the Act words which are not expressly included in it.[53]

It is important to reconcile the two, apparently contradictory elements in this passage. How is it possible to 'read words into' an act, whilst engaging in a task of 'construction'? From my review of the authorities, and I acknowledge this is not the only possible understanding of those authorities, the court may not supply words omitted by the legislature, *per se*. Rather, what a court may do is construe the words

---

[52] See *R v. Young* at [5]–[32]; *R v. PLV* (2001) 51 NSWLR 73 at [88]–[89]; Spigelman, 'The Poet's Rich Resource' supra at 233–234.

[53] *Jones v. Wrotham Park* at 105. This passage has been adopted and applied in a number of authorities: see those set out in *R v. Young* at [10]; see also *Mills v. Meeking* at 243–244; *Newcastle v. GIO* at 116.

actually used by the legislature *as if* certain words appeared in the statute. The words are notionally 'included' to reflect in express, and therefore more readily observable form, the true construction of the words actually used, by way of a strained construction.

I re-emphasise the words from Lord Diplock that I have quoted: the task of the Court 'remains one of construction'. In order to be able to characterise the process as one of construction – which remains a constitutional restriction on the role of the judiciary – it is best to avoid describing the process as one of 'introducing words into the Act'. It remains a process of construction only if what the Court is doing is to interpret the words actually used by the Parliament.

The issue of 'text' versus 'purpose' has been traced back to Aristotle.[54] The reformulation of a statutory provision with additional or fewer words should be understood as a means of expressing the Court's conclusion with clarity, rather than as a description of the actual reasoning process which the Court has conducted.

Interpretation must always be text based. As I have said above, the task is to interpret the words of the legislature, not to divine the intent of the legislature.[55]

In Australia, the basic authority on legislative inadvertence

---

54 Manning supra at 4.

55 See text at n 28.

is *Cooper-Brookes v Commissioner of Taxation,*[56] which in fact affirms the centrality of the text. The joint judgment of Mason and Wilson JJ stated:

> [T]he propriety of departing from the literal interpretation . . . extends to any situation in which for good reason on a literal reading does not conform to the legislative intent as ascertained *from the provisions of the statute*, including the policy which may be discerned *from those provisions*.[57]

In my opinion, *Cooper-Brookes* is not a case of reading words into an act. What the Court concluded was that in a particular paragraph, the word 'company' should not be given the extended meaning, which one section said that all such references should be given. In the full context of the whole act, and of the legislative history, the section which made provision for the extended meaning was read down so as not to apply to the specific reference in one paragraph.[58]

To similar effect is a later judgment of the House of Lords, *Inco Europe*, which, notwithstanding a statement about reading words into the Act, took words of general application, namely 'any decision of the court under that

---

56 *Cooper-Brookes*.

57 ibid., 321 (emphasis added).

58 *R v. Young* at [17]–[22].

Part' and concluded that that particular composite phrase had to be read down, so that the phrase 'under that Part' applied only to some sections in the Part.[59]

As I indicated above, Lord Diplock identified three necessary conditions before a court could undertake the process that he referred to as 'reading words into an act'. In *Inco Europe* these conditions were expressly relied on and the Court emphasised that such a process was limited to what could be characterised as 'drafting mistakes'. Lord Nicholls of Birkenhead said, in a passage worthy of extensive quotation:

> It has long been established that the role of the courts in construing legislation is not confined to resolving ambiguities in statutory language. The court must be able to correct obvious drafting errors. In suitable cases, in discharging its interpretative function the court will add words, or omit words or substitute words.
>
> . . .
>
> This power is confined to plain cases of drafting mistakes. The courts are ever mindful that their constitutional role in this field is interpretative. They must abstain from any course which might have the appearance of

---

59 See *Inco Europe Ltd v. First Choice Distribution* [2000] 1 WLR 586 esp at 592 noting the references to how a provision should be 'read' in the context of 'adding or omitting words' as part of an 'interpretative function'.

> judicial legislation. A statute is expressed in language approved and enacted by the legislature. So the courts exercise considerable caution before adding or omitting or substituting words. Before interpreting a statute in this way the court must be abundantly sure of three matters: (1) the intended purpose of the statute or provision in question; (2) that by inadvertence the draftsman and Parliament failed to give effect to that purpose in the provision in question; and (3) the substance of the provision Parliament would have made, although not necessarily the precise words Parliament would have used, had the error in the Bill been noticed. The third of these conditions is of crucial importance. Otherwise any attempt to determine the meaning of the enactment would cross the boundary between construction and legislation . . .
>
> Sometimes, even when these conditions are met, the court may find itself inhibited from interpreting the statutory provision in accordance with what it is satisfied was the underlying intention of Parliament. The alteration in language may be too far-reaching.[60]

This approach, which I understand to be the same as Australian authority that has adopted Lord Diplock's

---

60 ibid., 592.

three conditions,[61] constitutes genuine, rather than spurious, interpretation. References in judgments of Justice McHugh to a court giving effect to the legislative purpose 'by addition to, omission from, or clarification of, the particular provision' should be so understood.[62]

The radical application adopted by the House of Lords for the UK rights-compliant interpretation section, discussed in the second lecture, encompasses reading words into an act. In an influential judgment, Lord Steyn expressly referred to the application of s 3 of the UK Act leading to 'the implication of provisions'.[63]

In *Ghaidan*, Lord Steyn characterised that case as having 'read words into' the Act.[64] He said, authoritatively:

> Section 3 . . . is . . . apt to require a court to read in words which change the meaning of enacted legislation, so as to make it Convention compliant. In other words, the intention of Parliament in enacting section 3 was that, to an extent bounded only by what is 'possible', a court can modify the meaning, and hence the effect of primary and secondary legislation.[65]

---

61 See *Kingston v. Keprose* at 423; *Mills v Meeking* at 244.

62 See *Mills v. Meeking* at 243; *Saraswati* at 22.

63 *R v. A (No 2)* [2002] 1 AC 45 at [44].

64 *Ghaidan* at [29].

65 ibid., [32].

The Supreme Court of Canada has also adopted, admittedly in a constitutional context, a practice of reading into legislation words in order to ensure compliance with the Canadian Charter of Rights. This has been of particular significance with respect to the equality clause which prohibits discrimination on one of a number of grounds. It appears that the Canadian Supreme Court has adopted terminology from United States jurisprudence about the equal protection clause, which characterised legislation in terms of 'under inclusiveness' or 'over inclusiveness' for purposes of concluding that a statute had, respectively, failed to include persons who should have been included, or included persons who should not have been included.[66]

As the learned author of one of the basic texts on Canadian constitutional law has put it:

> An interesting phenomenon has been the Supreme Court of Canada's use of the remedy of 'extension', under which the court extends the reach of a statute that the court finds to be 'under inclusive'. An under inclusive statute is one that excludes some group that has a constitutional right to be included. Sometimes this is accomplished by 'severance', deleting from the statute the language that

---

66 See, e.g., Laurence H Tribe, *American Constitutional Law*, 2nd edn, Foundation Press, New York, 1988, pp. 16ff.

> excludes the group. Other times this is accomplished by 'reading in' inserting new language into the statute to add the excluded class.

Accordingly, in one case the Supreme Court of Canada held that a provision of the *Unemployment Insurance Act* 1971 which allowed more generous childcare benefits to adoptive parents than to natural parents was 'under inclusive', but the court stayed its hand from striking down the legislation so as to permit the government to determine whether to alter the law. However, the court asserted that it would have had the right to read in corrective terminology.

Chief Justice Lamer said:

> . . . extension by way of reading in is closely akin to the practice of severance. The difference is the manner in which the extent of the inconsistency is defined . . . In the case of reading in the inconsistency is defined as what the statute wrongly *excludes* rather than what it wrongly *includes*. Where the inconsistency is defined as what the statute excludes, the logical result of declaring inoperative that inconsistency may be to include the excluded group within the statutory scheme. This has the effect of extending the reach of the statute by way of reading in rather than reading down . . . It would be an arbitrary

distinction to treat inclusively and exclusively worded statutes differently.[67]

'Reading in' was regarded as an 'appropriate and just' remedy to provide for an infringement of the Charter, within s 24 of the Charter. I doubt whether Australian judges will follow these precedents, whether in the application of the principle of legality – with the enhanced salience many of the sub-principles are receiving – or in the application of rights-compliant interpretation provisions.

If I can again commit the sin of self-quotation:

> [87] The process remains one of construction if the words actually used by the Parliament are given an effect *as if* they contained additional words. That is not, however, to 'introduce' words into the Act. It is to construe the words actually used. Interpretation must always be text based. The reformulation of a statutory provision by the addition or deletion of words should be understood as a means of expressing the court's conclusion with clarity, rather than as a precise description of the actual process which the court has conducted.

---

67 See *Schacter v. The Queen* [1992] 2 SCR 679 at 698; 93 DLR (4th) 1 at 12–13.

> [88] The authorities which have expressed the process of construction in terms of 'introducing' words to an Act or 'adding' words have all, so far as I have been able to determine, been concerned to confine the sphere of operation of a statute more narrowly than the full scope of the dictionary definition of the words would suggest. I am unaware of any authority in which a court has 'introduced' words to or 'deleted' words from an Act, with the effect of *expanding* the sphere of operation that could be given to the words actually used . . . There are many cases in which words have been *read down.* I know of no case in which words have been *read up.*[68]

Notwithstanding some observations by Justice McHugh in the Court of Appeal, not repeated in his equivalent High Court judgments, the position in Australia is that identified by Justice Stephen: 'It is no power of the judicial function to fill gaps disclosed in legislation'.[69]

These observations must be read together with the judgments in *Cooper-Brookes, Jones v. Wrotham Settled Estates* and *Inco Europe,* to which I have referred. Indeed Justice Stephen subsequently said:

---

68 *R v. PLV* at [87]–[88].

69 *Marshall v. Watson* (1972) 124 CLR 640 at 648; See also *Council of the City of Parramatta v. Brickworks Ltd* (1971) 128 CLR 1 at 12; *Ruzicka* at [6]; *VOAW* at [12]; *Cornwell v. Lavender* (1991) 7 WAR 9 at 23.

> To read words into any statute is a strong thing and, in the absence of clear necessity, a wrong thing.[70]

The process must remain one of interpretation so that a reading of the text with additional words must be 'reasonably open', to repeat the overriding test from Lord Reid in *Jones v. Director of Public Prosecutions* and Mason and Wilson JJ in *Cooper-Brookes* quoted above.

Conclusion

I return in conclusion to the century-old article by Roscoe Pound which, again, merits extensive quotation because of its contemporary resonance. He said:

> . . . The bad features of spurious interpretation, as applied in a modern state, may be said to be three: (1) That it tends to bring law into disrepute, (2) that it subjects the courts to political pressure, (3) that it reintroduces the personal element into judicial administration . . . In the first place, in a modern state, spurious interpretation of statutes, and especially of constitutions, tends to bring law into disrepute. Law is no longer the mysterious thing it was once. This is an age and a country of publicity. It is no longer possible to impose upon the public by covering

---

[70] *Western Australia v. Commonwealth* (1975) 134 CLR 201 at 251.

> legislation with the cloak of interpretation . . . The disguise is transparent and futile, and can only result in creating or confirming a popular belief that courts make and unmake the law at will. Second, in a common-law country where questions of politics and economics are so frequently referred to the courts, the knowledge that courts exercise, or may exercise, a power of spurious interpretation subjects the courts to political pressure which can not but impair the general administration of justice . . . Finally, spurious interpretation reintroduces the personal element into the administration of justice. The whole aim of law is to get rid of this element. And, however popular arbitrary judicial action and raw equity may be for a time, nothing is more foreign to the public interest, and more certain in the end to engender disrespect if not hatred for the law. The fiction of spurious interpretation can no longer deceive any one to-day. The application of the individual standard of the judge instead of the appointed legal standard is quickly perceived, and is, indeed, suspected too often where it has not occurred.[71]

This analysis represents an exposition of a point of view which remains relevant a century later. It is not, of course,

---

[71] See ibid. 384–385.

the only opinion held on these matters. Clearly the interpretation of legislation cannot be held to be spurious if it occurs pursuant to an express Parliamentary mandate such as the rights-compliant interpretation provisions discussed in the second lecture.

Nevertheless, even in this situation there remains a restraint on the judicial role. With respect to the exercise of federal jurisdiction that restraint could raise issues under Chapter 3 of the Constitution. In the case of all Australian courts, the issue is one of what Chief Justice Gleeson calls, judicial legitimacy. As his Honour said:

> Judicial power . . . is held on trust. It is an express trust, the conditions of which are stated in the commission of a judge or magistrate, and the terms of the judicial oath.
>
> . . .
>
> The quality which sustains judicial legitimacy is not bravery, or creativity, it is fidelity. That is the essence of what the law requires of any person in a fiduciary capacity, and it is the essence of what the community is entitled to expect of judges.[72]

---

72 Murray Gleeson, 'Judicial Legitimacy' (2000) 20 *Australian Bar Review* 4 at 5, 11.

INDEX